The Haunting Himalayas

"...there is a misty vapor that encompasses our minds and hinders us from looking beyond the tangible – a fog that makes us doubt all else..."

Follow Rajni Sibal's journey into esoteric experiences with an amplified worldview. Once the mind is free from the shackles of rigid empiricism it allows for the truth of others. You begin to comprehend that what others perceive is not a mere myth simply because you do not.

'The Haunting Himalayas' is a collection of short stories based on real life experiences of eerie sightings, strange sounds and ethereal events. The book is an exciting sojourn across the hoary Himalayas which form a perfect backdrop. The core of these enigmatic narratives is at rue occurence. The author has woven enthralling stories around the core to craft a tapestry in which the warp and the weft are an exquisite mix of myth and reality.

The Haunting Himalayas is an ode to the pristine pine covered ranges.

The frosty mornings and rosy sunsets in the mountains heighten imperceptible facets of the cosmic truth. One sees better and begins to understand that *soft smudged line that separates the living from the dead*. The Haunting Himalayas opens up a fascinating vista of unknown dimensions and one learns to accept that there is more to the world than meets the eye...

The Haunting Himalayas

Rajni Sekhri Sibal

HAR-ANAND
PUBLICATIONS PVT LTD

HAR-ANAND PUBLICATIONS PVT LTD
E-49/3, Okhla Industrial Area, Phase-II, New Delhi-110020
Tel.: 41603490
E-mail: info@haranandbooks.com/haranand@rediffmail.com
Shop online at: www.haranandbooks.com

Published by Ashok Gosain and Ashish Gosain for
Har-Anand Publications Pvt Ltd

Printed in India at Vinayak Offset

To enchanting memories…
of misty winter evenings
and dusky mysterious skies
over snow-peaked mountains.

Formy children
Lakshi and Pushan
and
for Butanol
who stayed up with me through
long nights with an impenetrable
arcane look as he watched me write
mystifying tales through sleepy eyes
with an occasional wag of his tail…

Author's Note

"There is a fuzzy realm that separates the here and the now from what is ethereal…"

The astute words I heard at Tapovan spoken by an unlettered but wise man I met briefly at the end of an arduous uphill journey have stayed with me. His words helped me appreciate that there is more to the world than meets the eye – an important premise of this book.

In October 1986 I was part of a group of probationers who were sent by the National Academy of Administration at Mussoorie on a trek to Gaumukh, the source of Ganga. A trek in the Himalayas was a part of our training as civil servants. Four of us decided to hike beyond Gaumukh. We trekked up to the Gangotri Glacier and crossed over to Tapovan – a quaint high-altitude meadow encircled by picturesque snow-peaked mountains. I was soaking in the sense of peace that pervaded the serene environs when I met the sage who helped open my mind to accept truisms beyond empirically verifiable facts.

On returning to Gangotri we were informed that the man we had met was the '*Baba of Tapovan*'. No one seemed to know his name or where he had come from. None could recall when he arrived at Tapovan. That day, thirty years ago he bequeathed infinite wisdom to me speaking about seemingly innocuous things like the cobalt blue sky, the icy wind and the mountains around us:

"There is but a soft smudged line that separates the living from the dead... Just like this icy north wind, there is a misty vapor that encompasses our minds and hinders us from looking beyond the tangible – a fog that makes us doubt all else..."

Fear of the unknown diminishes when one begins to accept that life and death are merely loci along the same continuum. And a new vista of unknown dimensions opens up – especially as the bit about doubting the intangible is true for most of us. Well, it was for me before I realized that there are curious matters I know nothing about. As a student of science, I only believed all that I could see for myself or all that could be substantiated. There had never been any shades of grey between the black and the white for me.

My world had no room for uncertain probabilities...

Over the years I realized that the only valuable knowledge I ever possessed was that I knew so little. Thousands of years ago the Roman slave philosopher, Epictetus had said and I quote:

"...to know you do not know and to admit you do not know is a matter of courage ... and the beginning of all learning."

Admitting to myself that there was a whole world out there that I knew nothing about was the beginning of an exciting new journey. My worldview amplified and my mind allowed for the truth of all that others perceive in realms that are way beyond my ken...

Once I liberated my mind from the shackles of rigid empiricism I began to accept all that was hitherto imperceptible. I stopped brushing aside things I could not comprehend as mere myths!

The Haunting Himalayas is a collection of short stories that had bewildered me when I first heard them. The experiences narrated in this book are set against the backdrop of the Himalayas. During my years in the mountains I heard of many extraordinary episodes and mystical stories that were both fascinating and baffling at the same time.

Over the years I have stopped putting them through the litmus test of empiricism...

The enigmatic events in the book are based on true sightings. The occurrences have been shared with me either by the person who has experienced the incident or by a relative authorized to speak by the person. As the author, I have taken the liberty of weaving a story around the core to craft at a pestry in which the warp and the weft are an exquisite mix of myth and reality...

The myth is only peripheral and does not overtake the reality of the true experience. The conversations in the tales have evolved from my imagination. In some stories I have changed the names and in others the backdrop. Thus, the story titled Mulberry House Magnet is a true incident that happened in a Parsi family. But, the locale. and the names of the protagonist and other characters in the tale have been changed.

Sightings of a lady-in-whitehave been reported by trekkers near River Bhagirathi at Harsil in the Garhwal mountains and also near River Parvati beyond Manikaran as reported by Malini Shankar during her trek in the Parvati valley. The name Ishmylie Mem Sa'ab is a fantasy, as are Colonel Brampton and the other characters in the story. The conversations narrated in the story Ishmylie Mem Sa'ab are of my creation. I have also added a few twists and turns to enhance the narrative though the sensations and feelings as reported.

The poignant story of the love of a mother for her child is the basis of An Ethereal Call. The pain of her separation from her son travels across the Himalayas from Lahol Spiti to Mussoorie.

The Headless Soldier was sighted by Mrs. Kailash Kumari Mathur in 1938 as narrated to me by her daughter in law Madhuri Mathur. I have created a narrative around the true sighting of the soldier's head and taken the author's liberty to change names and shift the location to Camel's Back Road in Mussoorie under the British.

The Faquir who followed the protagonist at Joshimath is a true story with altered names. Some incidental elements of the experience as it is related in the book are a figment of my fantasy.

The words heart-liver-kidney stuck with me from a true event recounted to me when I was in School. The episode as it is related in the book did not take place in a school in Nainital. The backdrop of the story – a boarding school for boys beside a graveyard across Lake Naini – does not exist except in my imagination.

The Palkot story is true and has been narrated as it was experienced by the senior Thapliyal but I have embellished it with imagined conversations.

The story Tinkling Anklets has been crafted against the Chamba valley. The tale is based on a few recorded facts and some local myths about the Varman dynasty and the thousand-year-old disappearance of Princess Champavati – after whom the town Chamba is named.

Besides Chamba in Himachal Pradesh, the sound of tinkling anklets has also been reported hundreds of miles away from the Doon valley in Uttarakhand. The tinkling of anklets continued to be heard in Nasreen even after the building was taken over by a girls' school sixty years ago. The Orioles dormitory was abuzz with stories of the sound of anklets heard by many school girls along the corridor, which is now a portion of the library at Welham. An official complaint was made by Anjali Mohite's mother in the '70s.

I have never had any personal experience of a sighting. But I no longer consider events experienced by others as mere myths. The short stories in this book have true events at the very core. The nucleus is embellished with conversations and creativities to build a legend.

Welcome, dear reader to *The Haunting Himalayas*. The book takes you on a journey to an esoteric world of enigmatic events and legends. The canvas is wide and has been painted with enthralling events that course through the mountains – from a village in Lahol Spiti at the confluence of Chandra and Bhaga, through the hills of Shimla and Mussoorie, to Harsil on the banks of the Bhagirathi and on to Joshimath and Badrinath in Tehri Garhwal. The book then takes you on a voyage through time to the ancient kingdom of the Varmans in Chamba in Himachal Pradesh and right across to the Pauri Garhwal region of Uttarakhand with a short story set in a school in Nainital and an event that occurred in the pine forests near village Palkot.

Winter evenings in the misty Himalayas with snow falling outside makes the white world appear unreal and eerie – and a perfect setting for this book. There is nothing more charming than sitting around a fire made of pine logs with family and friends and reading or listening to stories that appear unreal in the warm amber glow of the fire. I have charming memories of several such evenings.

The Haunting Himalayas is an ode to the magnificent mountains and their treasure trove of magical mysteries.

The picturesque Himalayan ranges form the perfect backdrop to the short stories in the book. The pine trees and the purple hills lend a delicate fragrance to the tales. A moon that hovers just above one's outstretched arm imbues an ethereal quality to the environs. The mountains are pristine. The air is rare – and the star-studded sky heightens the imperceptible realms that we know so little about. Frosty mornings and rosy sunsets are the natural settings for charming sagas in the mountains...

Even as I write the author's note I distinctly recall a thought that struck me as I sat amid the hoary Himalayas on a trek to Har ki Doon, the valley of the gods:

"I am but a speck in time and space ...These mountains have been here before me and will be there after I am gone – a witness to so many incredible journeys..."

Indeed, the Himalayas have been silent spectators to eons of timeless events. Proximity to nature offers itself to heightened sensibilities. For some reason the unknown and all that is inexplicable becomes more distinctive in the mountains amidst falling leaves. You sense numerous facets of the cosmic truth and learn to accept that there is more to the world than meets the eye...

And it becomes apparent that there is indeed a rather fuzzy realm that separates the here and the now from what is out there in the ether.

As you turn the page to read the esoteric sagas from the mystical mountains, on behalf of the protagonists of all the arcane stories presented in this book, I would like to quote something a character states in one of the tales:

"I can understand how incredulous all this sounds to you. Well, I *saw* it with my own eyes and I *still* don't comprehend!"

Acknowledgements

I would like to place on record my gratitude to all those who shared their experiences with me and permitted me to use the sightings, their perceptions and the emotions that accompanied them for relating these esoteric sagas from the mountains.

A special thank you to Madhuri Mathur my teacher at School, who despite the excruciating pain in her knees spent hours telling me about the experiences of her now deceased mother in law Mrs. Kailash Kumari Mathur and other members of her family.

I am grateful to Mandira Mohan for sharing several experiences that formed the basis of the tales recorded in this book and to Rajesh for recounting the emotions some sightings in Ranikhet evoked in him.

My heartfelt condolences to the Rustoms who continue to mourn the bewildering and tragic loss of their son to a magnetic pull.

I thank Anjali Ane a childhood friend for allowing me to use her experience with the tinkling anklets at School and other sightings later in life.

My gratitude to Vijay Thakur, a *Chela* who recounted the myths around the disappearance of Princess Champavati after whom the town of Chamba is named and whose idol is venerated by some in the Champavati Temple. The story he told me at the *Minjar Mela* in the seventies has fascinated me over the years and has been retold here.

I thank Kavita Bahuguna for sharing her personal experiences that formed the basis of the story of the omnipresent sage.

I am grateful to my friend Sudarshan Paul Thakur for sharing the poignant story about a mother who doesn't know when she will see her child next and reaches out to him.

My gratitude to Rachna Dwivedi of the Thapliyal family for sharing the lore of the Palkot sightings.

I am grateful to Vikram Singh who shared his experience of sighting the lady-in-white at Harsil. I am also thankful to Malini Shankar for sharing her experience of a trek in the Parvati Valley and the emotions of some trekkers associated with sighting a lady-in-white on the river; and how a teenager from Pune had died all of a sudden in the river the night the lady-in-white was sighted.

I thank Narendra Kumar of Har-Anand Publications for believing in this book and urging me to finish it during the lockdown, despite commercial concerns post-Covid 19.

I thank Uma, my friend from School, for her beautiful oil on canvas which forms the perfect cover of this book and emotes the setting against which the esoteric experiences written in the book have occurred.

A special thank you to TK Manoj Kumar, a friend and colleague, for the frontispiece. The sketch of the Mussoorie hills enhances the book and adds a special touch.

Over the years, my two artiste friends, Uma and TK have become an essential part of most of my books.

I dedicate *The Haunting Himalayas* to Lakshi and Pushan who have been very patient with me as I have hammered at my laptop lost in a world of my own. Thank you Lakshi for helping me with the title. Pushan and Lakshi, you are both the inspiration for all the delightful things I have done in my life – like writing this book.

And last, but not the least, I thank Butanol who decided to sit up with me sometimes through the night as I wrote for long hours – his eyes drooping with sleep. He often looked up and gave a slight wag of his tail to show me that he was still awake and supporting my endeavor…

Contents

a smile is worth a lifetime...
for a smile lasts forever ... and more.

I

Ishmiley Mem Sahab

"This is an old story that occurred a hundred years ago... The story of *Ishmiley Mem Sahab* – Mili as she was called by all in these mountains. An ordinary girl with a beautiful smile..."

Bahadur paused as he looked around at the five eager faces of the young '*chhota sahabs*'. Their faces were glowing in the campfire he had lit to keep the October cold out. The youngsters were not like other birds of passage who merely crossed *Harsil* a quaint old village tucked away in the Himalayas.

Almost all those who passed through *Harsil* these days – pilgrims, adventurers and mountaineers – were in a rush to scale greater heights. Few paused to relax in the lush green meadows dotted with sheep. Most of them trekked up to *Gangotri*. Some even climbed a steep mountain beyond Gangotri to reach *Gomukh* – the glacier where the mighty Ganga was born.

The five boys on a trek in the Himalayas were not in haste. On a balmy October evening in 2018 they pitched their tents in Harsil and were camping on the banks of the cobalt blue *Bhagirathi* a tributary of River Ganga. They now sat around the fire listening to Bahadur their local guide with avid interest to his story.

Bahadur had related Mili's story umpteen times over the years to groups of trekkers who had camped at Harsil for the night.

He had to – for every time Mili had come down from across the river to meet the travelers ...

"She was a pretty *'pahadan'*. But the most remarkable thing about Mili was her smile... What a charming smile our Ishmylie Mem Sahab had!"

Bahadur paused for effect and saw me shiver despite the cold.

"It was an exquisite smile. Sunny and wide. You could never quite tell whether it was her lips that were smiling – or was it her soft brown eyes? Mili's smile simply lit her face up!"

'She hadn't smiled at me!' I thought to myself.

Beyond the fire Bahadur had lit for us, the night was dark and filled with eerie shadows. I trembled and drew my legs up. As I huddled closer to the fire I recalled the moment I saw an apparition coming out of the mist.

She had come to me like a soft breeze.

Clothed in white, she had looked ethereal in the moonlight. Her hair formed a halo around her face. I had stopped in my tracks and kept staring at her as if I was in a dream...

We, my four friends from college and I, had eaten an early dinner at the camp. After dinner I decided to explore the place. As I left I noticed that the others were preparing to go to bed. For, the next morning we were to start our climb to Gangotri early.

Bahadur had warned us against going out in the dark – and alone.

I ignored his blanket warning. When we asked him why not, he had merely shrugged.

"Just don't go out in the dark – and definitely not alone!"

Bahadur had repeated his warning as we went into our tents. The surest way of ensuring a teenager does something is to tell him not to without assigning a reason.

"What was he hiding? Why was he being so secretive?"

It was dark now. And I decided to check for myself – and alone.

I slipped out of the tent while the others were still packing their rucksacks for the next day. We were to trek up to Gangotri the next morning. As I left the camp I realized I had left my torch behind. There was no point going back. The night sky was filled with stars as it is in the hills. I felt I didn't need it.

My path was lit by a whimsical moon that played hide and seek with the clouds.

I must have walked for half an hour before I came to a rickety looking wooden bridge. The bridge spanned the river about a kilometer and a half upstream from where we had pitched our tents.

On hindsight I wish I had listened to Bahadur. But there I was standing on an ancient wooden bridge. An owl hooted from a tree behind me. A wolf howled across the river. And I sensed a presence.

I looked up and saw a lady in white slowly wafting towards me from across the river. A long white veil trailed behind her. She seemed to be floating – as if her feet were not touching the ground. She glided gracefully through the mist with her long hair flowing behind her and her white veil flapping in the breeze.

I stood transfixed staring at the enigmatic lady-in-white.

As she wafted towards me the moon went behind a cloud and I saw her silhouette sway towards me.

I felt a tug at my sleeve as a strong gust of wind removed the veil covering her face. The moon came out from behind the clouds just at that moment…

I looked up in horror at a faceless face!

I gasped for breath as I felt my throat constrict.

In the moonlight I saw the specter had a hollow above the neck surrounded by a glorious mane of long white hair.

There was no face – where a face should have been…

I screamed. But no sound came.

I heard a girl's voice whisper in my ear.

"Isn't the war over?"

And then with a rasping moan: "It's been so many years … the war must be over by now…"

I wanted to run. My feet refused to move – as if they were stuck in quicksand.

She gripped my wrist tight. I recoiled as I heard the apparition wailed.

"O it must be over! Where is my Bonnie sa'ab? Bring back my Bonnie sa'ab!"

All of a sudden, the apparition struck me with sharp long nails – nails that were sharp and shaped like the talons of a vulture. I felt her pointed nails tearing into my flesh.

I could neither run nor pull my arm away. I screamed in agony – but I heard no sound except the high-pitched voice of the lady-in-white screaming like a banshee…

"Why hasn't he come? You are from the plains, aren't you?"

Her grip on my wrist grew tighter. I felt warm blood oozing out.

My heart was in my mouth. My mouth went dry. My tongue was swollen thick. My eyes lowered, I dared not look up at that faceless face again.

Her voice acquired a shriller note and became more frantic with every word she spoke.

"So, if the war is over why has Bonnie sa'ab not come? Why are you here?... tell me!"

Those were the last words I heard.

I think I saw blood – maybe mine – dripping on the wooden planks of the bridge as I swooned and fell down.

I must have fainted. For the next thing I remember is looking up at Bahadur's anxious face. I felt cold water being splashed onto mine. I sensed, rather than saw, someone draping a blanket around me. Someone else forced me to sip warm sweet tea, which I think was laced with brandy. Bahadur had already lit a bonfire that was now roaring. I was warm as a toast but I was still shivering...

"Reaction!" I heard somebody say.

There was a searing pain in my right wrists. I looked down at the angry welts and the horrific experience I had been through earlier came back to me.

I shuddered as I recalled the lady-in-white-with-a-faceless-face!

The scratches on my wrist were washed and attended to. The only medical practitioner in the village had been brought to the camp to give me an anti-tetanus shot.

After I ate two biscuits and finished the oversweet tea, I settled down along. The others sat with me around the campfire Bahadur had lit – all eager to hear the remaining part of Bahadur's story about Ishmylie Mem sahib the girl with a 'charming' smile.

Bahadur told us how he had found me lying flat on the bridge. He had run along the bank when he heard one of my friends say that I had gone for a walk. He had panicked when he heard I was headed upstream and was alone. On reaching the old wooden bridge, he had found me on the edge of the bridge, where I had fainted. Another few inches and I could have been carried away by the swift rapids in the river.

I looked up with gratitude at Bahadur. The man had saved my life. He had picked me up and carried me on his shoulder for over a kilometer from the bridge to the camp.

"What happened Bahadur?" I asked nervously.

I saw Bahadur look away as if he could not meet my eyes.

"It couldn't be my imagination. I don't know who I saw or *what* I saw – but there was *definitely* someone!"

I put up my scratched wrist for all to see.

There was a pregnant pause and the only audible sound was the crackle of the fire as a log fell.

"It was Mili!" Bahadur said enigmatically. "Our Mili. She is a Harsil girl. She has been looking for Colonel Barrington for a hundred years now!"

We had all looked at Bahadur stunned.

"Mili? A hundred years?..."

"I told you all not to go out alone after dark – but all you '*chhota sahabs*' don't *listen*!" he said as he looked at me accusingly.

"Mili gets agitated! She gets restive only when she sees men from the plains. You see, she has been waiting for news from the plains about her Colonel's return after the War."

"Which war? What Colonel?" I heard someone ask.

"Wait! I'm telling the story wrong. I'll start at the very beginning...

This is an old story – the story of Smiley or Mili as she was called in these mountains. She was an ordinary girl who lived in Harsil long ago. An ordinary girl with an extraordinary smile...

The winter of 1899 was particularly cold and Harsil was snowed under. Mili was born on a frosty and dark night – the night of the lunar eclipse.

Sepoy Chand Singh, Mili's father was home on leave. He was in the British Army and had picked up a smattering of English. He was a bit of a '*Laat Sahab*' of the village.

When Sepoy Chand Singh walked down the village, everyone stopped to stare. He wore a solar hat and walked with a swag – an umbrella in one hand and a pocket dictionary in the other. He had received the dictionary as a prize for winning the marathon race in the Sepoy's Training School.

After he joined the Army, Chand Singh had made several valiant attempts to make his mother, Amma, call him Sepoy Chand Singh. But Amma had a mind of her own. She always used his childhood name – *Chandu*! And the entire village did too – much to Sepoy Chand Singh's annoyance.

Chandu took his first born in his arms and looked down at her. He did not know then that this baby would be his only child. The baby looked up at him and gave him a beatific smile.

"O just *look* at that lovely smile ... let us call her Smiley!"

Sepoy Chand Singh declared with a broad smile on his face.

"Ishmiley" repeated his wife, Gauri, with a lot of difficulty.

"Ishmiley" said Amma for the first and last time in her life.

Then Amma laughed loudly and air whistled through the gap in her front teeth.

"Don't do *git-pit-English* with me Chandu – I will call her Mili with love – just as you will *always* be Chandu to me!" she declared.

"Chandu's daughter Mili!" Amma smiled as she gently took the baby from her son and held her close.

Much to Chandu's annoyance, the whole village called her Mili.

Amma was rather worried that her first grandchild was born under a lunar eclipse. When she was younger, she had heard stories of ghosts and '*bhootanis*' and '*shledas*' coming down to the earth during an eclipse.

"All the dark forces reach up to the sky and dance around and hide the moon. That is why the moon hides it's face in an eclipse."

Amma repeated what she had heard her own grandmother tell her so many years ago. She looked down at Mili with fear.

"The village priest must be called – right away!" Amma declared.

"He will know what prayers are to be said to ward off the evil."

Pundit Govindji, the priest from the temple on the hill, was called within hours of Mili's birth. He brought out a sharpened rock and drew Mili's horoscope on the mud floor of the hut. Something in the intricate diagonal squares stumped him. He scratched his head.

"The eclipse is there. But I can't understand. The moon and all the planets seem to beam down on your daughter Chandu – in a very special way!" Govindji said a little perplexed.

Both Chandu and Gauri looked at the temple priest eagerly. "She is destined to shine brighter than the moon!" declared Govindji.

"Your daughter will rule over these mountains. She will be a proper '*mem sahab*' and even *you* will bow to her Chandu." Govindji chuckled at the look of joy on Chandu's face.

"*My* daughter? A *mem sahab*?" Chandu beamed.

Gauri touched her daughter's cheeks and laughed as she said:

"*Ishmiley Mem Sahab*! My little *Ishmiley Mem Sahab*!"

"Yes. Indeed, *Ishmiley Mem* Sahab!" repeated Pundit Govindji.

"She will have a long life. Your *Ishmiley* will live in Harsil forever!" declared the Pundit as he took of his spectacles.

"Forever?" said Chandu. "No one lives forever. We all have to die and burn on our pyres."

Pundit Govindji looked at the intricate squares he had drawn on the mud floor again and shook his head bewildered at what the stars said.

"No pyre for *Ishmiley Mem Sahab*!" he repeated solemnly.

He squinted as he peered at Ishmiley's horoscope.

"I don't know how! But she will live in these mountains forever."

A shiver went down my spine.

Bahadur paused. He looked at the eager faces of his audience, added another log to the campfire and went on with the story as all five of us listened with rapt attention...

And then Govindji, the village priest adjusted his holy thread. He peered at Chandu's mother. For Amma was the decision maker in the family. She always had been. Even when her husband was alive Amma had worn the pants in the house.

"Now let's talk about the special prayers Amma,"

"Ah! The pooja" Amma sighed as she gently put her granddaughter down and turned to the village priest – her little Mili who was to become a '*mem sahab*' and then 'one-who-lived-on-forever'.

"She doesn't need any special prayers. Your granddaughter

is a gift from the gods Amma. The stars declare that she will live at the feet of the goddess up on the hill."

Pundit Govindji told Amma who looked at him open mouthed.

Ten days later Chandu went back to his regiment headquartered in Dehra Dun in the plains. Mili was virtually brought up by the two women in the house – her mother, Gauri and her grandmother, Amma.

Years went by and Smiley, or Mili as everyone called her, grew up. Everyone forgot Pundit Govindji's predictions. Mili was a gentle young girl of fifteen when the Colonel first saw her.

Colonel Brampton, Chandu's Commanding Officer, was a keen mountaineer. A few months before the World War broke out, the Colonel was a transferred from Dehra Dun. Before he joined his new posting in Ambala, he wanted to trek in the Himalayas beyond Uttarkashi. Sepoy Chand Singh was chosen to be the Colonel's guide since he hailed from the area.

Together they rode on horseback up to Harsil, from where they were to trek uphill – a long and arduous journey. At Harsil, the Colonel was to halt for two days. The plan was to leave the horses behind and trek up to *Tapovan*, beyond Gangotri Glacier.

Chandu took permission to go home to stay in the village. The Colonel pitched his tents outside the village and camped on the banks of the Bhagirathi on *this* very site.

Colonel Brampton first set eyes on Ishmiley, our Mili, as she crossed the wooden bridge you met her on tonight *Saahab*.

I shuddered as I recalled my meeting with the enigmatic lady-in-white.

Bahadur added another log to the fire and continued his story...

Mili came out of the mist from the forest across the river with a small lamb in her arms. There was a heady fragrance of wild flowers about her. Her cheeks were flushed. She looked up as she reached the bridge and smiled. Her smile reached up from her lips to her eyes and produced two dimples on her cheeks along the way.

Colonel Brampton was smitten. It was love at first sight.

After that they met in the forest on the other side of the Bhagirathi. Mili would take her flock of sheep to graze across the river. The Colonel would follow. The two – our Mili and the Colonel – would cross the river and climb the hill below the temple. When they were not looking into each other's eyes, they spent hours looking at the picturesque vista and the splendid Bhagirathi flowing below.

Colonel Brampton's onward journey in the Himalayas kept getting postponed. Each morning before he left to go across the river, the Colonel would tell Chandu that they would leave the next day. It suited Chandu to remain home a little longer. Two days slipped into six.

Our Colonel was an honorable man, *chhote saahab.* On the sixth day he went to Chandu's small hut and respectfully asked Amma for Mili's hand. Everyone was delighted. Chandu recalled Pundit Govindji's prediction when Mili was born.

His Smiley was becoming a *'mem sahab'* indeed.

The whole village was abuzz. A *pahadi* girl marrying a Colonel!

Never had a *firangi,* a foreigner, and that too a *'bada sahab'* married a girl from Harsil. The two exchanged garlands before the gods and were married as per our customs.

Mili became Colonel Brampton's *mem sahab.*

'Madam Smiley' he called her. And to Mili, he was 'Bonnie Sa'ab'.

The Colonel's trek to Gomukh was abandoned. After they were married they lived together for idyllic eight idyllic days in the Colonel's tent on the banks of River Bhagirathi. They would cross the wooden bridge and explore the hills and the forests beyond. Their favourite spot was a spur below the temple. They dreamt of building a home there. They were both on cloud nine.

Eight days later the Colonel went away. Both Mili's husband and her father left the village the same day. Chandu returned to Dehra Dun and the Colonel went onwards to join his new assignment in Ambala.

Mili returned to her parent's house in Harsil.

To everyone who asked, Mili replied with a smile: "My husband, Bonnie Sa'ab, will return soon..."

But Colonel Brampton did not return. He never did.

The World War broke out on 14 July 1914 and went on for several years. Mili waited and waited for her Colonel Sa'ab for years on end. She lost interest in everything. She started spending most of her time on the spur below the temple. Mili would take the sheep to graze up the hill and spend the entire day there coming home only to sleep.

Mili waited endlessly for her Bonnie Sa'ab to come back and build their home on the hill.

The war got over but Colonel Brampton still did not return. Mili would go across the river to the site of their 'home' to wait for him.

Ishmylie was there the day her father Chandu came back from the war. As soon as he reached home Chandu went in search of his daughter. He bore the sad news of the Colonel Brampton's demise during the war.

Chandu saw Mili on the hill across the river with her sheep. He ran to the river's edge and hollered:

"Smiley! O Smiley! Come quickly – I'm home from the plains. I have news of Colonel Sahab!"

Mili ran down the hill forgetting her flock. She was rushing across the bridge her hair flying behind her when she tripped and fell into the roaring waters of the Bhagirathi. Before Chandu could do anything, the swift waters had swept his daughter away.

That was the last time Chandu saw his Smiley. In his anguish he did not even recall whether or not he had been able to tell his daughter that her husband Colonel Brampton was no more.

Chandu and his family never saw Mili ever again.

All of Harsil did … and continues to do so.

On cold misty days someone or the other sees Mili with her flock of sheep even now. Over the years, many villagers have seen her wandering in the hills across the river. She often walks along the bank of the Bhagirathi near this camp. Some people from the village have also seen her on that rickety wooden bridge – where she met *you* tonight Sir.

We see Mili from a distance. None of us has seen her up close. She doesn't speak to the hill folk. We have learnt to co-exist with the departed…

She seeks out visitors from the plains to enquire after Colonel Brampton.

The words of the lady-in-white I had seen on the bridge came back to me and the pain in my wrist seemed to increase.

"Isn't the war over yet? Where is my Bonnie Sa'ab? Bring back my Bonnie Sa'ab!"

As the sun was came up Bahdur's tale finished with the words:

"Ishmiley Mem Sahab lives on even after hundred years..."

No one slept that night. The next morning, we curtailed our trek and decided to go home – back to Delhi.

With the mountains behind us it all seemed like a dream.

My friends often wonder whether we had imagined it all. I do too until I see the welts on my wrist. Even as life goes on, I go back to that night in the Himalayas in my dreams and I wake up in a sweat.

Ishmiley Mem Sahab the lady-in-white-with-no-face haunts me still:

Isn't the war over yet? Where is my Bonnie Sa'ab? Bring back my Bonnie Sa'ab...

close your eyes and then see
for I will travel across the ether…

II

An Ethereal Call

"Tashi! Tashi Norbu Chang! Come here – let me touch your hair again. It is so soft…"

"Don't Ya. You will ruffle it into a messy mass. And I must get back now. The sun is coming up…"

"Yes, I can see it from I am. It is rising behind the mountains where the Tupchilling Gompa lies … You remember the Gompa?"

"Yes Ya. What a journey that was! I'll see you again but I must go now. Take care of yourself. I'm getting late … until next time Ya!"

"Until next time my dear Tashi Norbu…"

Dawn was breaking and the rouser bell at St Georges' School rang across the hills of Mussoorie on a balmy morning in 1968. Tashi realized that the Matron would soon be up and he would get into trouble if he did not rush. The grass was wet with morning dew. Tashi lay on his back and slid down from the top of the hill all the way to the spur where he fell into a patch of slush.

"O my goodness! Just *look* at you! What a ragamuffin you look."

Mrs. Russel, the matron of Cullens House, saw Tashi sneaking in through the side door and stopped him in the corridor, her eyes a perfect round behind her spectacles.

"Tashi it is only six! Exactly *where* have you been frolicking in the mud at this unearthly hour? No cross country run for you today. Get out of those muddy clothes. And then *you* Mr. Chang will come with me to the House Master – *right* now!"

Father Wright, the House Master of Cullens House, looked up as he saw Mrs. Russel march a scruffy looking ten-year-old into his Study. He was rather surprised, for Tashi Norbu Chang had never got into any trouble in all the four years since he had joined St Georges' as a boarder at age six. He asked the frightened boy to wait outside while he heard the lamentations of Mrs. Russel. Once she finished, he asked her to leave and to send Tashi in. Father Wright severely reprimanded the boy.

"What is *wrong* with you Tashi? Just look at your hair! How can you be so untidy? You are now the Sports Captain of Junior School. You have to set an example! *Which* world do you live in?"

Tashi lowered his eyes. Father Wright looked at the young untidy boy with his hair all over the place.

"You are *such* a bright boy. Always top of your class. And your Geography teacher tells me that the project you brought after the two-week summer vacation on the 'Rocks of Lahol' is so good that it is worthy of a college boy."

The House Master looked at the brand-new trophy on his wall.

"And son, *we* at Cullens House owe this Championship Trophy to you! We are *all* so proud of you on the sports field. But your Matron has *so* many complaints. Mrs. Russel tells me that ever since you came back from the break you leave the dormitory very early almost every morning and your clothes are spattered with mud when you come back. She thinks you probably slide down the mountain and roll in the mud!"

Tashi continued to look down at his unpolished shoes. He quickly rubbed the dust off one shoe against the other shin.

"If Father Wright sees my shoes I will get into a real flap!"

The House Master saw the slight movement. He walked across the table and looked down with astonishment at Tashi's muddy shoes.

"And look at those unpolished shoes! Looks like you have been walking through slush besides rolling down a hillside! Mrs. Russel says she initially thought you were practicing in the sports field. But apparently, you are out climbing the hill behind the chapel. That's bad! You know you are not allowed to go off on your own like this."

Tashi felt desolate. He hated being scolded and felt miserable. He had always been a favorite of the House Master and all the teachers praised him all the time.

"Only last week my Class Teacher Brother Williams praised me in front of the whole School at Assembly. Why is Mrs. Russel complaining to the House Master about me? There is no way I can stop. I have to go – I have to go when Ya calls me…"

The memory of Ya gave Tashi courage. He looked at the House Master straight in the eye and spoke without the slightest of nervousness natural to any other ten-year-old in his predicament.

"Father Wright please forgive me for my appearance. I will do *everything* you say Father but please do not stop me from going to the hill top. I cannot tell you *why* but I have to go! I will stop going so often. Please give me special permission to climb up the hill only on Saturdays please. I promise I will go before the sun rises and be back even before the other boys are up."

Tashi Norbu sounded very much in control up until then. He took off his shiny new badge of 'Sports Captain' and handed it to Father Wright trying to control his tears.

"Father you can take my Captain's badge away and I will undergo *any* punishment. But don't stop me. How can I stop when Ya calls me? – I just *have* to go when she calls..."

He looked up to see the House master looking perplexed.

"Father it is not fair! My parents can't visit me and I get no letters from home. *All* the boys get letters *and* phone calls. My mother is illiterate. My father is a '*Chauthi Jamaiti*'. Ba went to school for the first four years only for the '*Meethey Chholey*' and packs of four Parle G '*biscoots*' the government gave in Lahol to entice children to go to School. Ba has sent me with *great* difficulty to study at St Georges'... Father I *really* miss home...I miss it *so* much!"

Father Wright sat Tashi Norbu down and offered him a glass of water. He took a sip and set the glass on the table.

"Thank you, Father. The other boys in my class are my friends but they are so different from me. None of them seem to miss home ... I don't see my family till the winter vacations and then too only my Ba! I get no letters or calls and no one visits me. My village, Tandi, is hundreds of kilometers away and is snowed under half the year!"

Tashi gazed out of the Head Master's window at the gentle green slopes of pine forested hills with towering snow-peaked mountains in the distance. He sighed wistfully.

"Mussoorie is lovely but *my* Tandi is better Father! The Himalayas run *right* across to my village. I have often wondered if I jump from one mountain to another like a monkey I'll reach home soon!"

"Maybe you will Boy! But for god's sake don't try it this term! We have *just* made you the Sports Captain. I don't want to de-badge you for breaking bounds Tashi!" Father Wright guffawed.

He poured himself some tea bringing out a plate of biscuits for Tashi Norbu. The boy took one hesitantly and then soon polished off the whole plate.

"How are my Cullens' boys perpetually hungry? But Tashi Norbu Chang does sound rather troubled. I must find out what is bothering the child," mused the House Master.

"Now, sit down comfortably Tashi. I'll ask them to send up your breakfast along with mine. Let us have a nice chat Son. Tell me more about your family and your home. I am *truly* fascinated – your village sounds like a wonderful place."

"Yes, Father Tandi is so scenic that it feels like heaven!" Tashi said excitedly. "In Lahol Spiti we share these mountain ranges with Mussoorie but we live much higher. Tandi is 10,500 feet high. The temperature in winters touches minus thirty-five degrees. There is no electricity. We beat the cold with Yak wool blankets and bedsheets made of sheep skin. My village lies at the confluence of Chandra and Bhaga rivers from where the Chenab starts. Believe me Father when the sun rises across the Himalayas, the water in the Chenab turns amber and looks like gold with little sparkles of sunlight..."

Tashi looked out of the window dreamily and then turned his head towards the Head Master.

"You know Father we Laholis started coming down to Manali and other parts of Himachal Pradesh only after the Sino-Indian war, when trade with Tibet was stopped. We actually have a greater affinity with Tibetans. Our food habits, our features, the way we dress, our dances and even our names are common. At School some seniors tease me for my small chinky eyes and instead of calling me by my name Chang, they call me *Chink*!"

"That's a *real* shame Tashi! Wait let me call the Senior School Captain – this *must* stop!"

"No Father please don't. I am OK – it really doesn't bother me. I am not ashamed of who I am and Father I wasn't sneaking. I was merely telling you about us. Ba has taught me to take care of myself. We Laholis have a lot of grit! My village Tandi gets cut off in winters for almost six months from the rest of the world."

"Is that so Tashi?"

"Yes, Father! We fend for ourselves. There are no heaters like we have at School. The only thing that keeps us warm is the fire we build from willow trees and yak butter tea. We Laholis are tough and *never* complain... But I *do* have a problem Father. There is no way I can reach Tandi in winter as it is completely inaccessible. So I can't go home during our three-month winter break. The fortnight we get off from School in the summer is too short. I have not been able to go home for *four* years Father ... since I was only six!"

Tashi's voice cracked. He looked as if he was going to cry. Instead he looked up at his House Master and gave him a broad smile.

"But *this* summer break was simply *fantabulous* Father! Ba took me home. He must have spent a fortune to fly me to Bhuntar and then to hire a car that drove us to Manali and all the way to Tandi through Rohtang pass! Since I had to reach school on time I spent only three days at home – but it was *Supercallifajulistacally* Super!"

Father Wright smiled at the joy on Tashi Norbu's face.

"For the first time since I joined St George's I went to Tandi. My mother has *never* seen me after I was a six – the day I left home for Mussoorie to join St Georges'. Ba had to *actually* introduce me to Ya, my *own* mother..."

Father Wright had seen Tashi grow from the time when he was a lost six-year-old. He felt his heart wrench but kept a straight face.

"I spent only three days in Tandi with Ya. But those three days were simply super! *Now* I understand what the other boys have and I do not and it really hurts Father! I miss my Ya ... so many years of a mother's love have been lost..."

The House Master felt the child's pain.

"And now I *have* to go when Ya calls! Please allow me."

"Yes Son – try to go again in the mid-term break next summer. So how was Tandi this summer?"

"O great Father! We knew we had just three days together – and Ya had no idea when she would see me next. So, she did not sleep a wink! She knitted me a pair of woolen socks and made straw footwear for me to bring back to School at night. Ba told me that Ya gazed at me as I slept to store every feature of my face in her memory... In the morning Ya would ruffle my hair to wake me up before dawn like she does now. There was *so* much to see and so much to do!"

Tashi's eyes were moist as he remembered how Ya had shown him a stash of woolen socks of all the colors of the rainbow – mostly to fit a six-year-old. The socks clearly fitted an old footprint.

"I still can't believe that Ya had carefully preserved the imprint of my foot, which she had deftly lifted from the wet ground over which I had walked on the day I left for School – to return only after four years!" Tashi mused as he held back his tears.

He recalled his last day at home during the mid-term break.

"On my last day Ya took me to see the *Tupchilling Gompa* after a breakfast of buckwheat bread."

"A *Gompa*?"

"Yes Father. A Buddhist Monastery. We Laholi's have been Buddhists since the 7th Century when Padmasambhav came through the Tibetan route from the Swat valley."

"The visit must have been special."

"Yes. The Gompa is beautiful Father. But Ya took such a circuitous route to get there that my feet ached by the time we reached. We walked for hours through slushy patches in the fields from one village to another. All I remember of the Gompa is an amazing feeling of immense energy as I put my tired feet upto sit down to pray. I felt a flow of strength and vigor. The way back to Tandi was much easier for we did not go round and round in circles."

Tashi Norbu paused speculating whether or not to say any more.

"Most probably he won't believe me – not until I take him to the hilltop. But if I don't tell him he will prohibit me from going when Ya calls – and that is truly important!" Tashi thought to himself.

"Father I learnt about why Ya took me in circles through the slush on our way to the Gompa. She ensured that I had walked through recently irrigated fields so that my foot prints would get imprinted on the ground. When I left the next day Ya retraced the route we had taken. She touched my footprints and blessed me through the ether."

"That is such a charming story Son! Your mother must really miss you."

"She does Father. And I do too. Ya has no idea when we will meet again. So once the sun dried up my footprints on the ground she tenderly carved out the sunbaked imprints. Ya told me she left a set of my footprints in the Gompa and took a set home. She has kept them next to the smaller imprints she had saved when I last left Tandi at age six. And this morning when she spoke to me Ya said…"

"How touching Tashi! That's a mother's love for you… Wait! When did you say you spoke to your mother Son?"

"This morning Father."

"What on *earth* are you talking about? You, Chang have been sitting with me in my office since six thirty and it is almost time for breakfast now. There is no way you could have talked to her this morning!"

"Ya called me this morning Father. I spoke to her before I came to your room. She calls me and we speak on the hilltop before dawn. That's why I need you to give me special permission to…"

"Are you out of your mind boy! How can your mother call you from your village in the Himalayas? There is no telephone in Cullens House except in this room. And on the hilltop? … *What* are you saying?"

Father Wright was perplexed.

"Tashi Norbu Chang you are a serious student and an excellent sportsman. I have seen you grow from when you were a child. I am fond of you Son – such an honest chap! What *are* you saying? Stop imagining silly nonsense!"

Tashi broke down and started sobbing into his hands.

"Father, dear Father you *have* to believe me! You know I never lie. Why will I lie to *you*? Ya calls me before dawn… I hear her in my heart. I sense her calling. I am not lying Father please believe me…"

"Tashi is rather straightforward and has never lied before. What is this poor boy imagining?" he wondered.

"I *hear* Ya call. There is a strong power that rips my blanket off and drags my feet through the steep climb. I whizz through the forest effortlessly and reach the top of the hill in a jiffy ... it is as if I have wings on my shoes. Believe me Father I am not lying."

Father Wright stared at the distraught boy incredulously. He looked out of the window in amazement for the steep uphill climb to the top normally took an hour.

"Ya talks to me at the hilltop. She tells me that this hill is on the same wavelength as the Gompa near Tandi. I go up each time she calls. And when I reach the hilltop I discern the aura of Ya's presence. I can feel her holding my hand ... ruffling my hair ... talking to me ... laughing as the sun comes up. I sense Ya. I hear her! I talk to her! She is *there* Father!"

"What humbug!" Father Wright thought.

"Come with me and talk to her. Let me take you uphill tomorrow at dawn. Please Father hear my mother's call..."

The House Master looked up and saw the guileless candor on Tashi Norbu's face. There was a ring of truth in the boy's voice.

"What harm can it do? Maybe I should go with the boy once. I will show Tashi he is only imagining things. And that will be the end of this nonsense!" he pondered.

"Alright, Tashi go wash your face and let us have some breakfast. Tomorrow morning, I will come with you. But I am getting old now – so no whizzing up mountains for me Son!" he said with a smile.

"Yes Father! No Father – I mean I will walk with you at your pace Father. I will call you when Ya calls. Thank you *so* much Father!"

Tashi was so excited that he could barely sleep that night. He couldn't wait for dawn to take Father Wright uphill when Ya called.

The air was crisp and the sun had not yet risen when Tashi Norbu and Father Wright climbed the hill the next morning. The boy held the House Master's hand on the way up. Father Wright could sense that Tashi was controlling his urge to clamber up faster. As they neared the top he smiled and let go of the boy's hand gesturing him to go ahead.

Father Wright was tired when he reached the top. His ankles were beginning to ache. He was breathless as he climbed the last spur. The sky had an amber glow. The sun had not yet risen. There was a strong smell of Yak wool that almost masked the aroma exuded by the pine trees. Father Wright shook his head.

"How strange? Yaks in Mussoorie? I must be imagining it but it definitely smells like Yak skin. Now where is that lad? He's dragged me all this way and disappeared."

The House Master heard a sound from behind a willow tree.

"There he is! What gibberish is Tashi Norbu Chang muttering?"

Father Wright saw Tashi sitting cross-legged like a Buddhist monk on a rock beneath a willow tree. The sun's first rays filtered through the clouds and touched his face. He looked calm and serene as he smiled at something he heard. Then he looked up as he saw his house master and gesticulated to him muttering something in a language Father Wright had never heard before.

"House Master Ya... Father Wright Ya!" Tashi said to someone in the air.

"My mother Sir. Come sit here Sir. She will speak to you.

But she is illiterate. She doesn't know English. She speaks only our language – Bhotia. I will translate for you."

"Stop this nonsense! What rubbish are you..."

Father Wright was cut short as he was about to reprimand Tashi by a soft and gentle female voice that spoke in perfect English...

"Good morning Father Wright. This is Mrs. Dolma Norbu Chang – Tashi's mother from Tandi in Lahol Spiti..."

As the sun came up in the hills of Mussoorie, Father Wright the House Master of Cullens House at St Georges' School fainted hearing the crystal-clear voice of Tashi Norbu Chang's Ya.

A mother's call across the ether...

only the meek choose safe waters
those who have faith take on the mighty river...

III

Tinkling Anklets

Chhan-chhan-chhan ... Chhan-chhan-chhan...

Anklets tinkled in the pine forests surrounding the River Ravi. The sound echoed through the valley of Chamba.

'Chhan-chhan-chhan!'

All night – every night ... from the banks of Ravi through the *Chaugan* to the green slanted roof of the *Akhand Chandi* Palace...

"It's only crickets!" the Matron said on my first night in the palace.

"*Crickets*?!" I wondered. "Rather unlikely – more like a prankster."

In the year 1975, I joined the Government College in Chamba as a Lecturer in Biology. I was given the additional charge of Warden of the girls' hostel. This allowed me to live in a comfortable suite of rooms in the erstwhile *Zenana Mahal* of the *Akhand Chandi* Palace. The palace had been the residence of the royal family of Chamba, the *Varmans* for over two centuries. In 1973 it was bought by the government of Himachal Pradesh and converted into a college and a library.

Beyond the latticed windows of my rooms in the palace was a mesmerizing vista of the quaint town snug amid snowy peaks. Across the lush green *Chaugan* was the *Champavati* temple built by Raja Sahil Varman in the memory of his daughter Champavati, after whom the town was named Chamba. River Ravi flowed below. The snow-peaked mountains nestling the town were witness to historical facts, fables and myths.

Tinkling anklets that echoed through Chamba in the monsoons was one of them…

"The sound doesn't bother me! Probably it is a cricket or maybe a cicada," said the Matron.

"But it bothers *me*! The sound is particularly loud in my room. Sometimes it is very rhythmic as if someone is dancing."

"Come, come! You are letting your imagination run wild, Warden!"

"The bells on the anklets tinkle *chhan chhan* all night – every night! I put my pillow to my ears but I can't sleep at night Matron."

"Just ignore the sound!"

"No Matron it is more than just the sound. Sometimes I feel there is someone in my room. I get a strange sensation as if a person is staring at me sleeping. One night I got up from sleep with a strong feeling that someone was sitting at the edge of the antique four poster bed in my room. I woke up suddenly and saw the curtains on my door swinging violently as if someone had *just* rushed out and I heard the tinkle of anklets fade away…"

My words sounded odd to my own ears.

"It's only an insect that chirps at night in the monsoons."

"Seems highly unlikely Matron. Crickets and other insects sound different. I teach Biology. So, I should know!"

"*That* may be so Warden. But this is my second year in this college and I know Chamba. You *are* new even if you are a Lecturer!"

Matron showed me my place firmly ending further discussions.

The mysterious sound continued to haunt me each night: Chhan-chhan-chhan…

However, it didn't seem to bother the other girls either. Like the Matron they too assumed it was an insect. I did not dissuade them. The night my flower vase broke after I heard the anklets tinkle rhythmically, I was *truly* mystified. I called the Matron to my room to show the proof of the strange experiences I was having.

"Look! See that broken vase." I gasped. "The feet wearing the tinkling anklets were dancing in concentric circles. They knocked my flower vase off the table and broke it last night!"

"Relax Warden! There is no one. Maybe a group of these insects live in the false ceiling of your room."

"No, no. Not just in my room. At times I hear someone walking on the roof with anklets on her feet – sometimes she runs across too!"

I paused as I saw the sardonic look on the Matron's face.

"Could it be one of the girls from the dormitory playing a prank?"

"They wouldn't *dare* Warden! They will get expelled in no time."

"Well then what *could* it be? – it's a mystery!"

"No mystery. Just an insect in the rains. It stops after *Minjar*."

"… *Minjar*? What's that?"

"Oh! *Minjar Mela* is a charming festival of Chamba. The fair has been held every year during the monsoons for hundreds of years. The whole town comes alive for twenty-one days!"

"Really? That sounds interesting. When is it?"

"Well, the festival begins soon on the second Sunday of *Shravana*. A pageant starts from the *Akhand Chandi Palace* – our college. The procession goes around the whole town and ends at River Ravi. The '*minjars*' are offered to the river in the presence of all the gods and goddesses."

"But what's a *Minjar?*" I asked mystified.

"A *minjar* is a bunch of paddy leaves and some golden silk wrapped in red fabric offered to the Ravi. Before 1943 a buffalo was also sacrificed to propitiate the gods. A live buffalo was pushed into the river. The belief was that if the river carried the buffalo away and it drowned all the sins of the town were cleansed. Now a days only a *minjar* is offered."

"Fascinating! And you tell me these strange sounds will stop then?" I asked.

"Yes. The night after the gods return to their temples is when the 'monsoon insect' stops chirping."

"The gods? Where do the gods return from Matron?"

"O! Didn't I tell you? During the *Minjar Mela* idols of all the two hundreds of gods and goddesses of Chamba Valley are placed on chariots and are taken in a procession. The gods return to their respective temples on the last day of the *mela*."

She peered at me through her spectacles and smiled.

"This strange insect of yours will stop chirping that night – till the next monsoon!"

"*Definitely not* an insect!" I repeated firmly. "There is definitely someone who runs around the Akhand Chandi Palace wearing anklets at night. *Who* is it?" I insisted.

"You could ask a '*Chela*'. Maybe *he* can tell you." Matron smirked.

She informed me that most of the deities of Chamba had a *chela* apart from the temple priest. A *chela* was a *special* devotee.

"During the *Minjar Mela* this *Chela* character goes into a trance!" Matron said with a laugh.

She obviously had a low opinion of the *chelas*.

"Apparently he can convey the prayers of all to the deity. In a state of trance, he answers questions put to him – about the past and the future... You can ask him about the sounds you hear Warden."

That gave me an idea. There were so many places I hadn't seen in Chamba – so many traditions I knew nothing about. I took some leave and visited all the old buildings and the ancient temples of the charming town that was my new home.

Yet, I found no explanation for the sounds I heard the sound every night "...Chhan-chhan-chhan..." And then I met the *Chela* of the Champavati *Temple*. King Sahil Varman had built the temple for his daughter. It enshrines the idol of goddess Mahisasuramardini the avatar of goddess Durga.

"How enchanting!" I said aloud to no one in particular. "A symbol of a father's love for his daughter."

A man in a pure white dhoti kurta smiled at me and introduced himself as the Chela of Champavati temple. I asked him if he could tell me more about the temple.

"Sure. Though the Palace has been sold to the government *this* temple continues to belong to the Royal family of Chamba. A father built it for his daughter. But not out of love alone – there was an element of guilt too!"

"Why do you say *guilt*?" I asked perplexed.

"Many years ago – about a thousand – King Sahil Varman was anguished by the disappearance of his daughter

Champavati. He built a temple in her name to appease the gods – but also because he was remorseful."

We were seated in the courtyard outside the sanctum sanctorum amid beautifully carved pillars. He folded his hands and sighed.

"You see when Champavati disappeared she never came back. All that continues to remain in these mountains is the tinkle of her *ghunghroos* – many bells strung together like an anklet."

The chela stopped as he saw my eyes widening with wonder.

"I can see that *you* have heard her too!"

It was a statement rather than a question. I nodded in affirmation my throat going dry.

"That's rather odd! Tourists from the plains normally can't hear her. Only we *Chambialis* can ... except sometimes even outsiders up in the palace or at this temple hear Champavatis *ghunghroos*."

And from the way the Chela bent his head as if to hear better, I think he heard what I did from behind a pillar.

"Yes. She is here even now! You see, Princess Champavati comes back to Chamba every year during the monsoons. She comes down from wherever she is and walks along the Ravi. Every night during the month of *shraavan* she sleeps in her old room in the Palace."

I froze. I recalled the number of times I had felt an amorphous yet strong presence in my room and all the odd occurrences that kept me awake even as anklets tinkled chhan-chhan-chhan ... through the night!

"O my goodness! So, it is Champavati I hear every night at the Palace!"

"Are you living in the *Akhand Chandi* Palace?"

"Yes, in the Zenana Mahal. I work in the College as a teacher."

"Namaste Teacher ji!"

He said with folded hands and then revealed why I was being visited by someone who had lived hundreds of years ago...

"Champavati lived there before she disappeared that fateful night."

"She *lived* there? No wonder I hear her! I sense her! I feel her sitting at the edge of my bed... What do I *do*?"

I was truly alarmed now.

"Take this image and place it in your room. No harm will come."

I looked at the bronze statue the Chela handed me. It was a small replica of the goddess Mahisasuramardini worshipped in the Champavati temple.

"The princess is a devotee of goddess Mahisasuramardini. Over the years, Princess Champavati herself is also venerated here in Chamba as a *devi* – a goddess. Every year at the *minjar mela* she walks alongside the chariot of goddess Mahisasuramardini. Her anklets tinkle rhythmically as she dances before the Mother."

I gulped. Princess Champavati had lived in Chamba a *thousand* years ago. The chela was speaking as if the princess were alive!

"During the fair, I sense the princess. Other people can also hear her anklets – but only a *chela* can actually *see* Champavati dancing before goddess Mahisasuramardini!"

The chela was enjoying the effect his words were having on me.

"She dances in the procession all the way to the Ravi and disappears into the river with the first offering of the *minjar.*"

I listened raptly.

"Then the gods return to their temples. Princess Champavati goes away to come back after a year in the monsoons."

"O my goodness! But *why*?"

"She's not at peace Teacher ji."

The Chela turned to me with sad eyes.

"And when a spirit is not at peace in these mountains – then the spirit wanders..."

He paused to see if I was comprehending him.

"If you allow yourself to sense things you cannot see Teacher ji ... you will see that there is a very thin line between the dead and the living."

That sounded rather philosophical. I was keen to hear the story of Princess Champavati Varman who walked these hills – her anklets tingling behind her – for hundreds of years.

"Tell me about Champavati. Why is she *still* wandering the hills?"

Then as the sun began to set over the mountains, the Chela of Champavati temple unfolded the fable of the dancing anklets ....

"Princess Champavati was King Sahil Varman's youngest daughter who disappeared when she was fourteen.

Legend has it that Champavati was the king's favorite child. She was born after ten sons. The king called the princess '*Champa*' – a Magnolia flower – endearingly. King Sahil Varman even named his new capital Chamba after his darling daughter *Champa*!

The Varman Dynasty was established in the sixth century AD and sixty-seven kings had ruled it from Bharmour, a town deeper in the mountains. Three hundred years later in 920 A. D. King Sahil Varman shifted his capital to Chamba, a plateau in the lower Ravi valley.

Champavati was not yet fourteen when the royal family moved to Chamba. Along with her brothers, Champa was taught archery and horse riding. A Guru was brought from the plains to teach her classical music. The princess was very keen to learn to dance. King Sahil Varman indulged his daughter in all other matters – but dancing was unheard of in the royal family. Princesses did not dance!

The only women who danced those days were the nautch girls at the palace and the *Gaddi* women of the happy go lucky nomadic tribe of shepherds. They roamed the 'Gadaran' green meadows, in the mountains and came to Chamba with their sheep during the monsoons.

From her windows in the palace Princess Champavati could see the *gaddi* women dance in abandonment in the rain. The princess would watch them and follow their graceful steps in her room. Champavati was a natural dancer and learnt fast. She managed to get *ghunghroos* – anklets with bells – from her personal maid.

At sundown Princess Champavati would put on the anklets beneath her riding boots and ride across the wooden bridge on the Ravi. In a clearing in the forest on the left bank she would tie her horse to a tree and take off her boots.

Beneath the dusky sky with the silent mountains as her audience Champavati would dance to her heart's content with her anklets echoing in the forest: chhan-chhan-chhan...

Her dance in the forest was a form of devotion to her. Princess Champavati even at that young age was a devoutly religious person. She used to often visit temples almost daily to pray. Soon her visits to the temple declined. With every tinkle of her anklet Champavati felt she was ringing the bells of a temple for evening prayers.

Just above the bank of the river where Champavati danced, was the hermitage of a sage. The *ashram* was built around a large idol of goddess Mahisasuramardini the avatar of goddess Durga.

One day as the sage was walking back to the ashram from the forest. He stood transfixed as he saw Princess Champavati dancing to the rhythm of the cosmos.

There was something ethereal and mystical about her dance. As she finished the sage blessed the young girl. She was captivated by the calmness on the sage's face and the serenity in his eyes.

The next day Princess Champavati visited the *ashram* around dusk. There was a sense of peace the sage radiated. But most of all Champavati was simply enthralled by the lifelike idol of goddess Mahisasuramardini in the center of the courtyard in the *ashram*.

Every day she would reach the *ashram* in time for the evening prayers. And with pious reverence she would take off her riding boots, adjust her anklets and dance in vibrant exhilaration before the idol of the goddess ... chhan-chhan-chhan.

News reached King Varman that under the pretext of going for a ride his precious daughter had taken to visiting the ashram of a sage across the Ravi. The king could scarcely believe what he heard.

'My darling Champa – not yet fourteen! What is she doing? She has never lied before.' The king mused.

King Sahil was crushed. All sorts of negative thoughts kept filling his mind. You know how suspicion can literally kill you, Teacher ji!

King Sahil was convinced that his daughter was up to no good.

'This strange so-called-holy man must have enticed my little Champa. The wretched man must be taking advantage of her innocence!' he thought.

With every passing minute King Sahil got more and more agitated He was too furious to think rationally. He took a sharp dagger and hid it under his cloak. That evening when Champavati rode her horse across the Ravi, the King followed her at a distance. He shadowed her to the ashram. When he reached he heard the tinkling sound of *ghunghroos*: chhan chhan chhan…

King Sahil could hardly believe his eyes. His precious daughter Champa was dancing barefoot at the center of the mud-plastered courtyard. Her eyes were closed and her long beautiful plait was undone. Champa's hair were swirling around her and her arms were outstretched. She danced in concentric circles in a trance to the sound of *tinkling anklets*!

Raja Sahil Varman was incensed at the sound of the *ghunghroos* on his daughter's feet – the feet of a Princess of the royal Varman family! But what truly enraged him was the sight of an old sage with a long grey beard watching his little Champa with half open eyes. The man could as well be her grandfather. He sat cross legged under a tree in the courtyard with his back to the King. The sage did not hear the king enter. He sat with his hands folded enthralled by Champavati's dance.

"How dare he! How dare this dirty old man watch the Princess of the Royal Family of the Varmans dance with ghunghroos on – as if she were a nautch girl?"

King Sahil Varman was *livid* with rage.

He took out the dagger from his cloak, gave the war cry of the Varmans and plunged it into the sage's body.

Champavati opened her eyes and was petrified to see her father.

The fourteen-year-old princess did not look back as she ran towards the river as fast as her legs would carry her. The king followed leaving the wounded sage bleeding on the ground.

King Sahil charged after his little Champa with the intent of taking her back to the palace. He would snatch the anklets and throw them in the river.

'I will find a good match and get her married far away from this wretched old man – far from Chamba!' King Varman thought to himself as he ran after Champavati.

The frightened princess kept running until she came to the river – and when there was nowhere else to go she jumped into the Ravi with the last tinkle of her anklets...

The king shouted to stop her. But it was too late. By the time he reached the bank of the river there was no sign of his Champa. He jumped into the river and dived below the surface to search for her but to no avail.

King Sahil Varman was distraught with grief. He came out of the Ravi and dropped down on his knees on the banks of the river – his body shaking with deep sobs. He cried his heart out.

'What have I done? My little flower – my Champa!'

The heartbroken father beat his breasts and howled with anguish. He bellowed at the skies, at the mountains and then at the river...

After some time, the grieving king fell down and simply gazed at the mighty river that had taken Champa away. As the moon rose he recalled the sage he had stabbed in a moment of fury. He got up and rushed to the *ashram* hoping to reach on time to save the old man. But when he reached the sage's hermitage he was astounded.

The *ashram* was empty – the injured sage had vanished!

'The loss of blood after the dagger wound would have left him too weak to move ... and where is the pool of blood?'

The king was confounded.

'And he couldn't have died ... for where is his body?'

The old sage of the *ashram* on the left bank of River Ravi had disappeared into thin air without a trace!

There was no one in the hermitage to help the King understand.

Only the angry red eyes of the idol of goddess *Mahisasuramardini* the avatar of *Durga* stared back at him accusingly in the moonlight.

King Sahil Varman fell on his knees before the statue of the goddess and wept like a child for being suspicious without a cause ... for having no faith in his own daughter's morals – a daughter he loved beyond all else ... for allowing violent rage to overtake all reason ... for stabbing an old sage ... for the loss of his daughter...

'O my goodness! So, my dear Champa you were dancing before Ma? It was your Mother you were dancing for! How did I not see the idol of the goddess? Will there ever be a bigger sinner than me? Forgive me my dear Champa! Please forgive your father! Come back my little one – please come back...'

King Sahil Varman cried in anguish to the skies above as he prostrated on the mud-plastered courtyard of the ashram before goddess Mahisasuramardini. But Champavati never came back!

No one knows what happened to her Teacher ji.

Did the swift Ravi sweep Champavati away? Or did the princess save herself from drowning – for she was a good swimmer? Did she swim ashore further downstream to live with the gaddi tribe? Did she decide to live a free life and never to come back to the confines of the royal palace of Chamba? No one knows Teacher ji.

Princess Champavati of the house of Varmans disappeared more than a thousand years ago at the age of fourteen.

King Sahil Varman was never the same. He died a very sad man.

The night Champavati disappeared was the fifth day of the month of *shravan.* King Sahil heard a voice in his dream admonishing him for not trusting his daughter.

"You will never see her again O King" said the voice. *"All that will remain of your daughter will be the sound of the anklets you never let her wear. She will sway between the two worlds and the only thing that will endure will be the sound of her ghunghroos..."*

A sound that echoes in these hills for the last thousand years!

The Chela of Champavati Temple looked up at me as he finished his tale.

"So, Teacher ji you understand what I said earlier? King Sahil Varman ordered the construction of this temple – but not *only* because he loved his daughter but also with a deep sense of guilt."

"Thank you. I now see why Princess Champavati is not at peace."

I looked up at the statuette of a fourteen-year-old princess who was now venerated as a goddess in the temple.

"But a *thousand* years! When will she be at peace?" I wondered.

"I don't now Teacher ji... All I know is that Champavati will come wearing her anklets and dance with the gods at the *minjar mela* in Chamba *every* monsoon – until the Ravi flows!"

"And where is she the rest of the time? Where does she go after the monsoons?"

"I don't know Teacher ji. Somewhere in the hills. Sometimes the *gaddis* have heard her dancing amongst the sheep. Sometimes some villagers have heard her dance on the banks of the Ravi. At others she goes to the other realm – the one we know so little about."

Then the Chela looked around as if he was sensing something.

"She could be anywhere at *any* time. Maybe *even* now she is here in the temple where we pray to her..."

He paused and we both looked at each other.

I know that the Chela also felt what I did – a strong presence.

Someone got up from the parapet behind us – someone who had been listening to her tale being related after a thousand years.

And as she left the Champavati Temple we heard a distinct sound of the anklets on her feet tinkling: chhan-chhan-chhan...

what is it that draws me to you?
what is this pull you have on me...?

IV
The Mulberry House Magnet

Shernaz Mistry and I met in Shimla at Bishop Cotton, a boarding school for boys where I taught English Literature to the senior school. Shernaz taught the boys Physics. She had the quiet good looks that grow on you and a pleasant smile; but she rarely spoke to anyone. There was a certain sadness about Shernaz.

We were both made responsible for the annual concert at the School Founder's Day in October. Shernaz and I became friends over the month and a half we spent together: deciding the play, selecting the cast, identifying props and attending rehearsals.

One balmy evening, the rehearsal took longer than usual. As dusk fell I asked Shernaz if I could walk her home. The sun had set and it looked like rain. She looked up at the ominous clouds in the sky and nodded in agreement.

The Mistrys lived close to the Ridge for the last ten years. The family had moved to Shimla from Nasik when Shernaz was twelve. Her father was a manager in a bank. Faredoon and Frenni Mistry – her parents – had rented 'Mulberry House' a quaint bungalow.

Mulberry House was a good one hour's walk from the School. The winding path took us through a thickly wooded coniferous forest. We had barely walked a mile and a half when we heard loud thunder and it started raining cats and dogs. Wet and cold we ran into a gazebo – a 'viewpoint' built for tourists to take in the vista.

"Let's take shelter here" I urged Shernaz.

"No, no! I need to get home soon. My mother will be frantic!" she said.

"It's pouring Shernaz. We'll get drenched. Let's stay here until the rain lets up."

"Ok. I guess it makes sense," she sighed still looking concerned.

"Don't worry about your mother Shernaz. She knows that you will take longer to reach home in the rain. Plus she knows you aren't alone. You *did* tell her that I was walking you back when you spoke over the phone before we left – did you not?"

"Yes. I did. But she will *still* worry. My mother gets *simply* hysterical when we don't come home on time – Naoroze and I."

Shernaz rarely talked about her family. Her brother Naoroze was the only person I had met even though we were beginning to talk about marriage.

"She was never like this when we were in Nasik. Ever since Cyrus went Mummy has become very anxious..."

"*Cyrus?*" I asked quizzically.

I had no idea of who that was. Shernaz looked at me with eyes that appeared moist even in the dark.

"Cyrus was my little brother. He was a year younger than Naoroze. They were the best of friends and were always getting into some mischief or the other. Cyrus, was the naughtier one!"

"*Was...?*"

"Yes, Cyrus passed away a little after we moved into

Mulberry House." Shernaz said with infinite sadness in her voice.

"He was only seven!"

"What happened?" I asked gently.

Shernaz peered into the night looking for the right words to use.

"Cyrus died. He died under very mysterious circumstances... You will *never* believe how he went!" She said with immense sadness.

Then her eyes grew larger with perplexity.

"Something *truly* eerie happened that day! Something that has never happened before – or after either."

Shernaz looked up at me in tears remembering the ill-fated day her brother Cyrus had died at Mulberry House nine and a half years ago.

"All of us tried to pull him down as hard as we could – but we could not save Cyrus..."

Shernaz caught my hand and said softly: "I haven't told this to anyone. But I will tell *you* – I will tell you all!"

And on that dark cold night amidst the patter of raindrops on the tin roof of the gazebo Shernaz Mistry related the mysterious saga of the Cosmic Magnet at Mulberry House....

"You know that my parents shifted to Shimla when my father was appointed as Manager of his Bank. On arrival, he took some leave. Every morning my parents would trudge through Shimla searching for a house to rent. After a week they came upon a perfect home to bring us up – the three Mistry children. I was twelve, Naoroze eight and Cyrus the baby of the family was not yet seven.

Mulberry House was just-the-right place for us! A white bungalow with green gables and a green coloured tin roof. The house had extensive gardens with hydrangeas and derived its name from the seven mulberry trees at the edge of the garden. There used to be a tall Deodar tree in the backyard.

The highpoint was the rent quoted by the owner S. Tandon. It was so low that my father could scarcely believe his ears. He wondered why anyone would want to rent out a brand-new property at such a low rent. Mummy had pushed his apprehensions aside.

'It *is* beautiful! Stop overthinking. You *always* overthink Faredoon!'

My father signed a rent deed for ten years. The terms suited S. Tandon, who was a trader from Delhi. He had built Mulberry House as a summer retreat for his only son, Jagan, who passed away before the construction was complete.

Jagan Tandon was a brash young man who was given to drinking. He used to drive up to Shimla to supervise the construction. A tragedy occurred on his last visit. He disappeared under suspicious circumstances and was last seen having a spat with a construction worker at Mulberry House. A year later Jagan Tandon was presumed to be dead although there was no trace of his body.

Mrs. and Mr. S Tandon were devastated. Due to the emotions attached to the house they did not want to sell it but still wanted to have little to do with either Shimla or the house. The Mistrys were the most suitable tenants and a long-term tenancy of Mulberry House was the best solution in S Tandon's view.

We were the first occupants of Mulberry House. Mummy loved her new home. The house was close to Papa's bank and he often walked home for lunch. I lost my heart to the garden.

After School, I spent hours reading beside the hydrangea bushes – when I wasn't helping Mummy in the kitchen.

My brothers, Cyrus and Naoroze, would drop their satchels as soon as they came home from School and would rush out to play in the garden. Climbing the mulberry trees was their favorite pastime. The trees were short and the branches were low enough. Once they had managed to climb the tallest one, the mulberry trees no longer offered a challenge to them.

The boys often longingly eyed the tall Deodar tree in the backyard with its inviting wide branches that spread out like a lyre. Even the lowest branch was too high for them to reach. Mummy had warned Cyrus and Naoroze about climbing it. The boys dared not disobey Mummy. The Deodar was just outside her kitchen window!

One Sunday afternoon, Cyrus ran excitedly to Naoroze.

"Let's climb the Big Tree today."

"How? Mummy will *kill* us!" Naoroze the more obedient one said.

"I just saw her go upstairs. She's got a headache."

His face cheerful like the cat who has been at the cream, Cyrus pulled Naoroze towards the large Deodar tree in the backyard.

"But I can hear someone in the kitchen," said Naoroze cautiously.

"O! That's only Shernaz finishing lunch that Mummy started to cook. Don't worry – *she* won't snitch. Shernaz is a *good* sport!"

"OK. Let's go – but quietly. Shush!"

Naoroze warned Cyrus as he saw his younger brother stretched his right arm up to the sky getting ready to whoop with joy.

The Deodar proved a difficult nut to crack. Naoroze could jump up and reach the lowest branch but Cyrus could not, however hard he jumped. The boys circled the tree to find a way out. They found a mound of solidified cement probably left behind by the construction workers. The elevated mound was under a low hanging branch of the tree on the side distal to the kitchen window. Cyrus discovered that if he climbed onto the mound and stood on his toes he too could climb the Deodar.

My mother walked into the kitchen looking fresher after her nap before I could warn my brothers.

'Where are the boys? There's too much silence. I am sure they are up to some mischief! Just *what* are these boys up to?'

'I think they are trying to climb trees ... maybe the tall deodar...' I said a little nervously with one eye looking outside the window.

Naoroze was already halfway up the tree. Cyrus was close at his brother's heels, gingerly trying to find a good foothold.

"*What*? It's too tall! Why didn't *you* stop them Shernaz? I am really very angry – I had clearly told them not to climb that one," she said crossly.

Mummy was terribly worried! She stuck her head out of the window and hollered at the boys. By then they had reached the higher branches.

"Cyrus! Naoroze! Come down *at* once! I want you off that tree now. *Right* now!"

Hearing their mother shout the boys panicked. Frightened they let go of the branches and jumped.

Naoroze landed on his feet on the grass. He turned around to help his younger brother.

Cyrus should have landed close to the raised cemented mound.

But he did not... Cyrus was hanging in thin air!

Mummy rushed out of the kitchen flapping her arms and shouting on the top of her voice.

I followed stumbling and screaming like a banshee.

"Cyrus! Cyrus! O my God – What's happening? Cyrus!"

Papa was sitting in the front garden with his newspaper. He ran to the backyard hearing the loud shouts and screams.

He too was stunned at what he saw...

Our dear Cyrus was suspended midway between an upper branch of the tree and the ground below – defying the laws of gravity!

His arms and legs were flaying and thrashing all over the place.

Everything was a big blur. A peculiar magnetic force was pulling Cyrus up towards the sky!

"Frenni jump! Catch him! Grab his arm. Hold on hard Frenni!"

Mummy jumped up to catch Cyrus's left arm and tugged at it as hard as she could.

"You too Shernaz! Pull him down by the other arm." Papa shouted.

"I've got his legs. There's such a *strong* force pulling him up. I am pulling as *hard* as I can but I can't seem to bring him down alone. Both of you pull harder – with all your might!"

"What's happening Faredoon? What's happening to our baby?" Mummy said between sobs.

I heard my mother muttering the '*Ashem Vahu*' under her breath. Papa joined her and so did I. We prayed and pulled Cyrus down at the same time. Even Naoroze grabbed on to my waist and tugged. We recited the '*Ashem Vahu*' on the top of our voices and pulled Cyrus down with all our might!

Cyrus stayed afloat in the air above the raised cemented mound.

The harder we dragged Cyrus down the stronger was the magnetic force pulling him upwards.

The gravitational force of the earth and the combined weight of all the Mistrys was up against a mightier opposing force pulling Cyrus upwards.

All of a sudden for no ostensible reason the upward force stopped – as if the current in an electromagnet was switched off.

All of us Mummy, Papa, Naoroze and I fell down with a thud.

Cyrus slumped down to the ground with his feet hitting the cemented mound under the deodar tree and became unconscious.

Papa and I tried to revive Cyrus frantically as Mummy ran indoors to call an ambulance with a Doctor. By the time the ambulance reached Snowdon Hospital, Cyrus was no more…

Cyrus was declared dead on arrival at the hospital."

I looked at Shernaz befuddled by the story I had just heard. Nine years after Cyrus Mistry was pulled up by an inexplicable anti-gravitational magnetic force under a Cedrusdeodara, the Mistrys can hardly accept he is no more or fathom how he went.

"An upward magnetic pull? A nebulous force opposite to and stronger than gravity? How is that possible?" I thought to myself

"But I don't understand! How could that be? What did the Doctors say?" I asked bewildered.

"Well, the Hospital conducted a postmortem. The autopsy revealed no cause for Cyrus's death. He was a normal healthy seven-year-old!" Shernaz said, raw pain writ on her face.

"Magnetic pull *opposing* gravity? Shernaz it is mind-boggling!"

"Believe me! We pulled Cyrus with *all* our might! I felt the strength of the force with *these* hands!" Shernaz put up her hands for me to see.

"Even after nine years we can *never* forget that terrible day – the way he went! He was barely seven – our little Cyrus…"

Shernaz wiped her tears as the rain stopped. We headed back to Mulberry House. We were silent until we reached the Ridge. She turned to me as we neared her house with infinite sorrow in her limpid eyes.

"And you know what? It's so odd! The macabre force was never witnessed at Mulberry House – either before or afterwards *ever* again. It's as if the magnetic pull manifested itself that terrible day only to take away our dear Cyrus…"

As I turned to walk to my house I felt Shernaz's pain engulf me. There were so many questions I had about the magnetic pull of Mulberry House – questions I didn't have the heart to ask her.

Later that week Naoroze divulged some other mystifying facts.

He informed me that a couple of days after Cyrus passed away the Police had come to Mulberry House to investigate. When they heard the about the magnetic pull, they called some construction workers to cut open the mound of solidified cement.

A human skeleton was found inside the cemented mound on which Cyrus had stood to climb the Deodar tree.

The skeleton of a man in his twenties was tangled in the cement. It appeared that someone had been buried alive in liquid cement, which had solidified later.

The skeleton was found to be of Jagan Tandon, who was last seen near Mulberry House before he disappeared mysteriously. The Police handed the skeleton to the Tandons, who performed the last rites of their son.

The skeleton in the mound under the Deodar tree was cremated.

The Deodar tree at Mulberry House was cut down.

A scientist I shared details of this event with found no explanation for this obscure phenomenon.

The magnetic force at Mulberry House that defied gravity and pulled Cyrus Mistry upwards and then threw him down to his untimely death remains a mystery to this day…

a puff of smoke and I fly on a cloud
knocking softly on heaven's door...

V

Tobacco on a Rock

There is no scientific or logical basis for what I am about to relate to you. You may not believe what I recount.

But believe it you must – for it is true!

I know it is true because I heard it from my father, Satyavachan Thapliyal who was orphaned as an infant. He was brought up by his paternal grandmother and grew up in Palkot a village in the Himalayas in Pauri Garhwal, where he is known as 'Satya' or truth – a value he stood for his entire life.

On a cold winter night, Satyavachan Thapliyal narrated something he had never talked about but had never quite forgotten. I was home from the boarding school I went to in Pauri, the biggest town near Palkot. My school was shut for winter vacations and I wanted to go out to play with my friends. My mother forbad me from going outdoors. The weather department had predicted a snowstorm in the region. The sky looked grim and my father agreed with her.

"Your mother is right Son. You need to stay indoors."

Although I pleaded with my father with all my might I knew it was of little use. I pleaded. I cajoled. I did everything short of throwing a tantrum. He was at his wit's end. There is little a man can do to keep his energetic eleven-year old boy entertained when he wants to go out to play in the snow.

Satya decided to relate a curious tale from his childhood – a conundrum that still puzzled him.

"This happened a long time ago when I was about your age, Son..."

He looked at me quizzically as he weighed his options.

"Should I or should I not relate the episode. He's too young to understand – not that I understand still!"

He built a roaring fire and called out to my mother.

"Shanti! Come here. I want to tell you both something I saw with my *own* eyes when I was Alok's age."

Mother came in with two cups of tea and a large mug of warm milk with honey for me. We sat around the fire as it grew dark too engrossed in the saga that unfolded before us to notice that a blizzard was raging outside.

"I have analyzed what happened that day ever so often but I still don't comprehend. Maybe *you* can help me understand, Alok..."

"Wow! You need *my* advice?"

My father was of a scientific bent of mind and very well read. And here he was asking *me* – a mere slip of a boy – to help him appreciate something that *he* could not fathom himself.

I was fascinated and charmed – no truly *kicked*!

"This is a true story..." my father said.

"You don't have to say that Satya!" my mother interrupted. "When have you ever told a lie?"

"OK Ma. Stop! Please let Baba tell the tale..." I urged.

"This happened when I was a sturdy lad of twelve – a little older than you are now, Alok. There was never a good School in Palkot."

"So where did you study, Baba?" I asked.

"My grandmother sent me to study at Messmore High School."

"You studied at Pauri? As a boarder like me?"

"Yes, he was a boarder. But the schools then were tough. Your father had to go home to Palkot *every* weekend for his rations."

"That's true Shanti"

"And I am certain it wasn't easy for you Satya! The bus from Pauri did not go all the way to Palkot then. There was no connecting road to the village. The bus stopped at the main road. Your father had to walk several miles up one hill and down the other to reach home... Things were *very* difficult then, Alok!"

My mother was on her favorite topic! She loved telling me how easy things were now and how tough life was in the hills in *their* times. But that was all my mother knew about the strange events my father related that night. Like me, she too was hearing the tale for the first time...

"Your mother is right, Alok. Every weekend I had to walk for miles on end to get to Palkot. And as you are aware every mile in the hills feels almost as long as two in the plains.

One weekend the bus from Pauri had a break down on the way. The driver dropped me rather late in the evening at the point on the main road from where I had to climb up to Palkot through the forest.

Clouds were beginning to descend and the sun was about to set. It would soon become dark. As I walked further I heard some eerie noises that I could not decipher. Once I even heard the howl of a wolf at a distance. I hurried along to cover as much distance as I could.

Two hours later I stopped to catch my breath after a particularly steep climb. I sat on a rock and opened my water bottle for a sip of water. My thirst quenched, I turned to look at the path I had covered.

I sensed rather than saw someone behind me.

There was a rustle of leaves and through the foliage, I saw the silhouette of a tall figure wearing a long overcoat and a top hat. I could not see his face. The hat was pulled down low. Smoke was emanating from a pipe sticking out from under his hat…"

Satya paused and turned to his wife.

"You know me Shanti," he said. "I am not a nervous person. Nor do I have a wild imagination."

"Yes. That's true!" She nodded in agreement.

"I found it rather strange. *Who* wears a top hat and a long coat while climbing a hill? But what *really* bothered me was why was he smoking? The jungle could have easily caught fire… *Who* in his right mind smokes in a forest?"

"Yes, that's odd. No *pahadi* – a person from the hills – would! Must be an outsider" my mother agreed.

"Even though it irked me that the stranger was smoking a pipe, I did not call out and tell the man in the long coat to stop smoking. After all, I was far from home and too young to get into a spat with a grown-up man in a forest. But I decided to keep away from him.

I got up to rush ahead of the stranger and maintain a fair gap between us throughout the walk. The man started walking behind me. I kept my eyes glued to the path and kept tramping ahead.

After sometime, I was surprised to see that the stranger was walking ahead of me! I don't know how! I had presumed that I had left him far behind. Although I hadn't seen him cross my path, at some point of time during our uphill climb he must have overtaken me.

A little later the stranger in the long coat and top hat was behind me again. Later, I saw him ahead of me. This went on for a while. The man in the top hat was ahead of and behind me several times. As I recall the event even *now* I have no recollection of him crossing my path *even* once! Nor do I remember overtaking him.

But there we were – the stranger and I, playing a strange form of tag in which neither of us crossed each other's path as we climbed the hill to the top!"

My father looked at my animated face. I didn't realize that my eyes had become round with wonder.

"Then the path descended downhill into the valley towards Palkot. As I turned a bend, I heard the most beautiful sound a tired hiker can in a forest – the sound of running water.

A stream was gurgling past small stones and pebbles. Since it was not yet summer, the glaciers had not melted and the stream was quite shallow with large ferns growing on both sides. A few wild daisies had sprung their heads up between the ferns...

I paused in my journey to marvel at this beautiful sight. Taking off my shoes and socks, I put my feet in the stream and allowed my toes to luxuriate in the ice-cold water. Feeling refreshed, I was putting on my shoes to cross the stream when I heard a rasping voice behind me.

'Please help me cross over.'

The sun had almost set. Even without looking around I sensed that the stranger in the hat and long coat was behind me

– the one who had been playing invisible tag with me for the last forty minutes.

There was no moon in the sky. As I turned around to face the stranger I could only see his profile in the dark…

'Yes. Of course, I will help' I whispered softly.

Although I felt a strange creepy sensation down my spine I held out my hand to help the stranger walk across the stream.

'No carry me across! I can't walk in water.'

The request of the healthy grown up who walked straight-backed surprised me. I couldn't see him but the man appeared to be too heavy for me to carry. I was barely twelve but I was sturdy. Those days I had a stubborn never-say-die attitude..."

"You still do!" My mother smiled as she interrupted his story.

"Yes Shanti… So, even though I was certain I would never be able to, I bent to pick the stranger up in the dark … I was surprised at how light he was – much lighter than even my satchel!"

"O my *goodness*! How is that possible?" I couldn't help exclaiming.

"I too was astonished, Son. When I crossed the stream with him on my back I was astounded at how easy it was. The stranger who was almost twice my height weighed like a feather…"

I gasped and felt my mother's arm around my shoulder.

"As we reached the other side, the stranger told me to put him down by the stream.

'Good! Put me down on that big flat rock at the edge of the stream. And leave!' said the stranger in a long coat.

'That was rather rude!' I thought. *'He didn't even thank me.'*

As I walked home I wondered at how such a tall and hefty looking man could weigh so little! How could he walk uphill wearing a long overcoat and a top hat? And how had he gone ahead of me and then behind me and then ahead again – without ever crossing my path.

My grandmother was worried and was waiting for me at the door when I reached home. She said nothing when I narrated the incident to her and merely stroked my hair tenderly.

Then holding both my hands in her own she told me that the stranger I had seen was no stranger to Palkot. Many a villager had seen the man in the coat and hat smoking his pipe in the jungle.

'He likes his tobacco they say!'

Before we slept that night, my grandmother lit an earthen lamp. Folding her hands in the form of a '*pranam*' she bowed her head. She was of the firm belief that there was no need to go to a temple to pray – for the gods were all around us in the Himalayas.

The next morning, I woke up early to play with my friends. After breakfast, I was already out of the house when my grandmother stopped me with a strange request. She looked around to see that no one was listening and handed me a small pouch.

'Satya, before you go to play do something important for me. Take this pouch of tobacco. Place it on the rock where you dropped the stranger you carried over the stream last night – the one with the long overcoat and top hat.'

Though I was disappointed for the chore would take me half a day, there was no way I could ever say no my grandmother.

"Remember one thing – you *must not* look back!"

She placed the pouch in my hand and warned me once again.

'He must be out of tobacco again! Just place the pouch on the rock and walk back home. Do *not* – and I repeat *not* – look back under any circumstances!'

I was rather bewildered by the firmness in my grandmother's voice as I picked up the pouch.

Except for the steeper portions, I ran for a great part of the three-kilometer hike to the stream. I wanted to return to Palkot early and didn't want to waste my holiday on delivering tobacco to strangers.

By the time I reached the stream I was tired. I sat on a rock to catch my breath and realized it was the same rock where I had put the stranger down the previous evening. I felt a niggardly feeling that I wasn't alone. Someone was close by. I heard a rustle of leaves as if someone was treading the ground tentatively...

'Gosh could it be a leopard in the jungle? And so close?'

But no one had ever seen a leopard on this particular hill. The un-defined sensation of being watched did not go away. I quickly did my grandmother's bidding and placed the pouch of tobacco neatly on the rock.

As I turned to go I heard the clear sound of fallen leaves being trampled over. My grandmother's words came back to me:

'Remember you *must not* look back! Just place the tobacco on the rock and come home – and do *not* look under any circumstances!'

The words aroused my curiosity. I was only eleven. Her

telling me not to look back repeatedly is what enticed me to do exactly that!

I walked a few yards and hid behind a tree. From behind the trunk I saw a figure approach the stone.

An hand reached out and picked up the tobacco pouch – the hand of a skeleton…

I shrieked on the top of my lungs and dashed home!

The pouch was dropped. The bone of a forefinger pointed at me.

I *ran* for my life and did not stop until I reached Palkot!"

My father looked dazed as he finished his extraordinary tale. My mother sat open-mouthed and I shuddered…

"A Ghost! Gosh Baba!" I gasped as my eyes growing bigger.

"You *actually* carried a ghost on your back! And you gave him tobacco?"

My mother gulped nervously.

"…*Was* it a ghost Satya?" she asked incredulously.

"No Shanti. I don't know – I know nothing about ghosts… All I know is that I have given you a factual account of what happened. Every word is true!"

I shook my head in disbelief and realized that I was holding on to my mother's hand.

"Wow! ... So, not a ghost! … But you *did* carry him! You carried a tall man in a long overcoat and a top hat who 'weighed like a feather'! Those were your very words… And you *saw* – *actually saw* – with your *own* eyes a *skeleton* pick up a pouch of tobacco from a rock!"

"I guess it sounds bizarre Alok!"

"Not bizarre Satya, but definitely strange."

"Even to my own ears it sounds rather incredulous! But believe me it happened just as I recounted it, Shanti. It happened to me – and to some other people in Palkot I am told!"

"I believe you Satya – we both do," my mother said and smiled nervously at me holding my hand. "But what a story – gosh…"

The fire had almost died down in the fireplace. The world looked dark and disturbing and a storm was raging outside our window. As I slipped into bed that night my father's words haunted me…

"A skeleton stretched an arm and picked up the tobacco pouch!"

The next day I recollected the story my father had related the previous night and thought to myself: *"What a hero my father was – even at my age! I wonder what I would have done!"*

I recalled what my father had told me.

"I know nothing about ghosts … but it actually happened with me … and with some other people in Palkot I am told…"

Nothing seemed as sinister as it had the previous night. I broke open my piggy bank and collected all the money that I had saved. I went down to the only cigarette vendor in Palkot and bought a pouch of tobacco for a pipe.

Around dusk I walked up to the stream in the jungle.

As the moon came up I put the pouch of tobacco on the flat rock by the stream in the jungle near Palkot and waited behind a tree till the moon came out from behind a cloud and…

I will follow you till the end of time
to the end of this world and beyond...

VI

The Faquir who Followed Me

"Where do I begin to tell this story?"

We were sitting in my mother's room at Joshimath, a small town nestled in the Himalayas. I was visiting her along with my children during their winter vacations. Ever since my father passed away my mother was all but bed ridden. The doctors had diagnosed her cancer rather late. She had very little strength but she loved to spend time with Varun and Varuna, her grandchildren.

My children had pestered her to tell them a story from the hills – a 'true story'! I propped her up in her bed till she was comfortable. She smiled as she started relating a strange but true personal incident – or an '*aap beeti*' as she called it.

"At the beginning...?" said Varun, my eight-year-old son said trying to be helpful.

"The beginning is a good place to begin Nani" Varuna, his younger sister piped in.

My mother smiled lovingly at her favorite grandchildren.

"Yes dear. The beginning! Only I really don't know *when* exactly the *Faquir* came into my life."

Smiling at their avid faces my mother related a story that even I had never heard before...

"I was not yet fifteen when I got married to Nana, your grandfather.

Two days after our marriage Nana went back to his unit in the army. The house was full of relatives and guests. They had stayed back for a week after the wedding. My father in law a Manager in a factory near Dehra Dun left a week later.

Soon it was just the two of us in this ancient ancestral house – my mother in law, Amma, and I.

That's not strange in the hills. Most men go to the plains to work leaving the women behind to run the home and take care of the children. My new home in Joshimath was ancient and felt spooky once the wedding guests left. It was all a little strange for me as I came from a rather large household in the valley in Dehra Dun. My father and his two brothers lived with their families under the same roof. The already full house was perpetually filled with visitors and relatives from the hills.

My new home was large and vacant. The five rooms on the first floor of the house were locked up. Every nook and cranny seemed ominous. I felt lonesome in this enormous old house and got frightened easily. I had a rather wild imagination those days!

Dusk was the favorite part of my day. At sundown when the bells in the temples rang I would rush up to the terrace. I loved the feel of the sun's last rays on my face before they lit up the snow peaks on the mountains beyond.

A fortnight after our wedding I saw the *faquir* for the first time!

One evening I was on the terrace watching the setting sun. Before the sky grew dark a bright full-moon appeared – a little yellowish like fresh milk. The moon was so close that I felt that if I stood on my toes and extended my arms up high enough I could have touched it!

I leapt up playfully as if to touch the moon. Strong and sturdy arms restrained me as someone pushed me backwards and I fell on the terrace. Rubbing my scraped knee, I was shocked to see that I was almost at the edge of the terrace. Another step and I would have fallen off the parapet. I turned around to thank my mother in law. But there was no one. The terrace was empty. Yet I could sense someone – someone who had saved my life…

Puzzled, I looked at the hill across from our house. A rather hazy apparition caught my eye. I peered and saw a long scarf flapping in the wind. A fuzzy image of a man wearing nothing but a loin cloth appeared to be sitting cross legged on the hill opposite our house.

He must be freezing. It was a cold October night. I was shivering even in my woolen shawl.

That night I dreamt that I was standing in a snow-covered meadow. A *faquir* attired in only a loin cloth was sitting cross legged on a snowy mountain. His eyes were shut tight. There were frozen icicles around his long-matted hair. The north wind didn't seem to disturb him. Walking up the mountain I took off my brand new red-quilted coat and draped it around the *faquir*.

I woke up with a start and felt the warmth of the sun's rays on my pillow.

The first thing I did that morning was jump out of bed and open my almirah. I was relieved to see my brand new thick red coat trimmed with fur hanging there neatly. My brother who was studying to be a barrister had brought the coat as my wedding gift from England.

I went downstairs in search of Amma, my mother in law. She was in the kitchen supervising the morning tea. Amma could see I was agitated and took me by my hand to the verandah. As she sat on her rocking chair I put my head on her lap. Amma ran her fingers through my hair as I related the events of the previous night.

"Don't worry. Strange things happen in the hills – especially when the moon is full…"

Seeing the look of horror in my eyes Amma held both my hands in her own and said: "Strange is not always bad, my dear girl!"

"You are in Joshimath, the holiest of holy places. Why should you worry? Every year Lord Badri's idol is brought here from Badrinath, higher up in the Himalayas. Joshimath is the lord's winter home. The idol is placed in the Vasudava Temple for the winter."

Then she looked at my downcast face and added: "There is still time for the Lord to come down. Let's go on a holy pilgrimage. Cheer up. We will go to Badrinath – just you and I!"

A week later we travelled to Badrinath – Amma in a *palanquin* – and I on foot. Amma's helper followed along with his cook and his provisions on a pony. Unlike these days, there was no bus or car that went up to the temple. One had to walk along a narrow path that passed through thick pine forests.

On the way up there were some very steep portions where I wished I had listened to Amma and hired a pony for myself too. We passed through some tricky portions where the path was narrow and had a sheer drop. I had to turn my face to the mountain and edge my way forward. A wrong foot could very easily prove fatal.

After two long and tiring days we reached the summit late in the evening. The doors of the temple at Badrinath were built of weathered wood and were shut for the night. We had to wait till the next morning to meet the Lord.

We camped for the night five hundred meters from the temple which shone in the fading sun against the sheer beauty of snowy mountains. Before I entered our tent for the night, I walked up to the temple. I stood outside the closed doors on aching legs and wondered what was so special about this place – why had Amma made me walk so far.

As I turned to go back I felt as if someone was watching me. It was dark and the feeling was eerie. I looked back at the temple and saw that the gate was now slightly ajar. A soft warm light from an earthen lamp was radiating through a slit. It was mesmerizing.

I'm not sure, but I think I saw him sitting there – cross legged with his back towards me on the steps of the temple at Badrinath – the *faquir* I had seen on the hilltop opposite our home in Joshimath.

Was I seeing things? Or was this man following us?

That night it snowed. Much sooner than expected. Everything was white and pristine the next morning. Amma and I were part of the last group to visit the temple for the year before the temple doors were shut for the winter and the idol taken down to Joshimath.

I looked for the naked faquir in vain. In my mind I hoped he had put on something warm by now.

We left Badrinath straight after visiting the temple. Amma said we should cover as much distance as possible before it grew dark. We had barely walked for four hours when the sun was covered by portentous clouds.

'O dear! It smells of snow!' said Amma.

Having spent her whole life in the hills, Amma could smell rain and snow before they appeared. And she was right! A strong wind started to blow and before we knew it snow started falling.

I took out my brand new red quilted coat trimmed with fur and zipped it up. The red fur lined hood protected me from the chilly wind.

We reached a part of the path which had been washed away earlier that year in a landslide during the monsoons. A wobbly wooden log had been placed over the gaping hole to act like a bridge. Beneath the log was a sheer drop into the valley below. The path had been tricky on our way up. With fresh snow the log had become slippery and dangerous.

Amma's *palanquin* had gone ahead and was waiting on the other side. As I gingerly stepped on the slippery log-bridge a mild whiff of pines engulfed me. At the same time, I felt an odd sensation at the nape of my neck. I could sense the presence of someone crossing the log behind me. The sensation made me nervous and the log wobbled beneath my feet. I turned to stop the person and lost my balance.

I heard Amma scream: 'Careful!'

Surprisingly, I did not topple down into the valley. I could feel *someone* holding me up and putting me back firmly on the log.

"Good you got your balance back in time! You could have fallen. Take care dear." Amma shouted.

I had not got my balance. Something – someone – had held me up and stopped me from falling... Yet there was no one behind me.

I heard Amma saying her prayers under her breath as I started walking along the slippery log.

I felt light-headed and shaky in my knees. But somehow, I crossed over sure-footed and without a hitch!

Amma seeing me reach the other side safely on light and sure steps, commented on my newly found mountain legs. She laughed and said: "Now my dear girl, you have become a *Pucca Pahadan* – a true girl-from-the-mountains!"

I smiled back and gave her a hug but I *knew* that was not true. The seemingly sure-footed person was definitely not me!

I had nothing to do with controlling my balance and preventing an inevitable death. Nor was it I who later walked across the log with the sure-footedness of a '*Pucca Pahadan*'!

I could not understand what had happened. There was no way I could explain it to Amma. I felt as if I was walking in the air and *someone* was supporting me amidst a soft aroma of pines.

Someone stopped me from falling off the cliff. *Someone* held my hand and helped me walk over the log safely to the other side.

There is no way I could have told Amma all this – no way anyone would have understood!

The snow came down faster and slowed our progress. I felt warm and snug in my new red fur-trimmed coat. Before it got dark, we reached a cavern and decided to halt there instead of pitching our tents for the night. A large rock at the entrance sheltered us from the north wind and protected us from the inclement weather.

After dinner the cook left a fire burning outside the cave. I was tired and my eyes started drooping. Soon I was sound asleep.

Around 2 AM I woke up with a start. A soft aroma of pine trees engulfed me. I felt someone staring at me from near the entrance of the cave. A chill went down my spine and I shivered as I heard the howl of a wolf. Then in the glow of the dying fire outside the cave I saw him again: the *faquir* I had dreamt of a full moon ago … the apparition I had seen on the mountain top in Joshimath … the person I imagined on the steps of the temple at Badrinath!

The *faquir* was sitting cross-legged with his eyes shut and hands on his knees in *dhyan mudra* – a typical meditative posture – on a bank of snow.

The *faquir* was completely oblivious of the storm raging around him. He wore nothing except a loin cloth and a cotton scarf loosely draped around his neck. His matted hair glistened with snowflakes. The chilly wind seemed to make no difference to him.

I put on my red coat and went out of the cave. The wind was tugging at my fur lined cape. As I approached the *faquir*, the spicy smell of pine cones became stronger.

I called out and asked if he was cold. I think the *faquir* knew I was there for I saw a movement on his closed lids. There was a gentle smile on his face but he did not respond or open his eyes.

Something in the way he sat alone on the snow moved me.

I took off the red quilted coat trimmed with fur that I wore and draped it around the *faquir*'s thin shoulders.

A minute before I took off the coat I had felt a twinge of unease. All sorts of strange thoughts entered my mind:

'How can I to part with my lovely red coat? It is so pretty and I have barely worn it for a day! My brother gave it with so much love and went back to England straight after the wedding. God knows when I will see him now!'

I pushed all such thoughts away as I took off my beautiful coat and draped it around the *faquir.*

'My need is less than this poor old man's. He will surely freeze in the cold if I don't give it to him!' I thought to myself.

I shivered all the way back to the cave. Huddled under the thick quilt Amma had brought for the journey, I slept peacefully for the remainder of the night – like I had never slept before!

The next morning Amma had to give me a good shake to wake me up. We had a long day ahead of us. So, we started early. There was no sign of the faquir outside the cave. He must have left earlier I thought, as we started walking home. There was a soft smell of pine wood – as is to be expected in a pine forest – but it somehow felt special.

The weather packed up around six that evening. We were caught in a snow storm. A blizzard was raging both ahead of us as well as behind us…

Amazingly, there was a circle of calm immediately around us – like a person experiences in the eye of a cyclonic storm.

All of us were astonished but no one said a word! As we walked on the *circle of calm* continued to envelop us and make way for us through the raging snow storm.

Amma saw me without my coat and asked: 'Where is your coat?"

"I don't have it." I said as close to truth as I could.

"But I saw you wear it yesterday! Have you left it behind?"

I nodded without saying a word. I shivered with fear hoping I was not in any trouble.

"Silly girl! You must be freezing. Here, take this shawl. It will keep you warm."

I refused saying I wasn't cold – and *surprisingly* I was not!

We reached Joshimath late that night. I went up to my room to take a warm bath. As I opened my almirah to take out my clothes, I was shocked at what I saw.

My red-quilted coat with fur trimmings was washed and ironed and hanging neatly on a hanger in the almirah – with a lingering smell of pines!"

"*Gosh*! Nani where did that coat come from?" Varuna asked her grandmother in wonderment.

"I don't know dear. Indeed, '*strange things do happen in the hills'* like Amma used to say!"

Mother wore a mysterious smile as she quoted my grandmother.

"*What* Nani? That man – this faquir guy – must have come back ahead of you and returned your coat to the servant in the house. What else? *What* Mystery Nani? No mystery!" Varun my son said.

My mother ruffled Varun's hair and smiled enigmatically.

"No Varun. He did not. Nobody in the house has ever seen the faquir! Not *even* Amma."

Turning to me she said: "But your father has! The first time he saw the faquir was in Singapore – the time he fell sick and was alone in the hospital. We were all so worried remember?"

I nodded remembering.

"Yes, I was expecting Varun. And Amma was sick in Joshimath too. I was almost in labor and unable to travel."

"There was no way I could leave Amma alone and go all that way to your father. I couldn't be in two places at the same time and was worried stiff. One night the faquir smiled in my dream and told me your father would soon be home. The hospital discharged him the same day and he came home in two days – a day before Amma passed away."

"*Really* Nani?" Varuna asked wide eyed.

"Yes dear. But what is truly amazing is that your grandfather also saw the faquir smiling and sitting cross legged on the edge of his hospital bed in Singapore at the *same* time that I saw the faquir in my dreams here in Joshimath! Even the doctor who discharged him an hour later, commented about the fragrance of pine cones in the hospital room."

"Aroma of pines in *Singapore*? What Nani? That's a new one! There are no pine trees in Singapore. *Everyone* knows that!" Varun piped in again with a laugh.

"That is marvelous isn't it? The *faquir* can be in the different places at the same time. And he carries the mountain air with him where ever he goes!"

Varun's eyes opened wide in amazement.

"Did you see the *faquir* again Nani?"

"Yes. He comes each time I am in trouble – each time I need him. Sometimes I see him. Sometimes I don't. But I know he is there. There is always a faint fragrance of pines when he is around..."

"Remember when your father had his open-heart surgery in the Army Hospital in Delhi? When the Doctors said his chances of survival were dim."

"Yes, I do. The doctors were shocked that he survived. He lived twelve healthy years after that." I said.

And then I remembered another strange thing.

"And Ma, there *was* indeed a distinct smell of pine trees in the ICU that day. I recall that so vividly."

"But there are no pine trees in Delhi Mom!" Varun asked incredulously.

"Yes, Varun that's true. There are no pine trees in Delhi. And there are no pine trees in Singapore either..."

I looked at my children and back at my mother again as I tried to figure things out for myself. I know for sure that there was a strong aroma of pines in the ICU when my father had recovered after the doctors had given up. I know because I smelt it myself!

"Gosh! Strange but true."

Ma smiled as she saw my disbelief change into a belief of sorts.

"Amma was right eh? Strange things *do* happen in the hills!"

That night my mother passed away in her sleep. Although her cancer had spread and was detected in the last stages but she suffered no pain. She went at dawn at home in her own bed at Joshimath when the sun was rising in the Himalayas and the temple bells were chiming.

She had spent her last night on earth with the three people she loved the most – her daughter and her grandchildren – relating the tale closest to her heart: 'the story of a faquir who followed her and stood by her through thick and thin like a true friend!'

She went as she would have wanted to go – peacefully and with a gentle smile on her face.

The next morning as I came into my mother's room I was flooded with memories. Looking at her lying cold on her bed I was overcome with grief and wept uncontrollably. Not only had I lost my mother, I had also lost my best friend.

I cried my heart out as I sat by her bedside on her favorite rocking chair. After a while, I felt spent and leaned back in the chair. As I shut my eyes I sensed a numbness at the nape of my neck.

I felt a strong presence proffering a sense of calm tranquility – like a warm blessing…

My grandmother's words in my mother's voice from the previous night rang in my ears and I felt a gentle hand stroke my hair as my mother had done each time I felt low.

"Strange things happen in the mountains!"

Startled I opened my eyes and the feeling was gone.

Yet, a lingering fragrance of something familiar followed me the whole day – a faint aroma of pine trees...

That day ... and whenever I felt low and needed a friend later in life too...

so how do I live without my heart…
give back what you took away from me.

VII

Heart Liver Kidney

"Heart. Liver. Kidney!"

Neil heard a senior student at St Thomas' Boys School whisper.

'The three vital organs in the human body!' Neil thought to himself for no apparent reason.

"Heart–Liver–Kidney! Heart–Liver–Kidney! Heart–Liver–Kidney!!"

All the other students ragging Neil in the Senior Boys' Common Room chanted in unison.

Neil looked at their fierce faces. There were eight of them. They looked almost sinister in the moon light streaming in through the window. It was enough to scare any thirteen-year-old.

But Neil was made of sterner stuff. He was born in the forests of Madhya Pradesh where his father was a Forest Officer. He had grown up with all forms of wild life and was fearless. That evening he did not allow his eyes to flicker and stared back confidently at the boys ragging him on his first day at School.

Neil was a dreamy boy and had a rather fertile imagination. Although he loved forests, he had always wanted to study in a boarding school in the hills. His parents had given in to their son's desire. They had driven up to Nainital, a town in the Himalayas, built around a natural crescent shaped freshwater lake. The town is bustling with activity and had several residential schools for boys and girls. Saint Thomas Boys' School was a boarding school situated beyond the graveyard that was built on the other side of Lake Naini.

Neil unpacked his trunks and met some boys from his class in the dormitory who took the new boy around the School.

"New comer?" a stocky senior asked as he passed the group of boys chatting in the corridor.

"Come to the Common Room below the Seniors' dormitory after dinner tonight!"

"Be careful. They'll rag you!" a boy standing close to Neil said.

"That's Ok. We have all been ragged at some point of time or the other. They'll only tell you to sing a song or dance or polish ten pairs of shoes. Just do what they ask you to do," advised another.

"But don't be cheeky! Or else they'll really give you a very difficult punishment" chipped in a boy who wore spectacles.

"I'm not scared!" Neil retorted.

"I don't care if they are seniors. They dare not ask *me* to polish their shoes or any such thing!" He added with firm determination.

The group surrounding Neil looked at each other in dismay.

"I will complain to the teacher…"

Neil's next words were inimical and totally unacceptable at Saint Thomas' – in fact in any Boarding School. Telling tales was an absolute no-no!

The junior boys feared that Neil's attitude would get him into trouble with the seniors.

Ragging at St Thomas was a way to get to know a new boy – although it was banned in the School after what happened that evening.

After dinner a boy of class nine was sent to escort Neil to the Senior Boys' Common Room where eight seniors boys were waiting for him. Neil told them his name but refused to dance to the latest western pop song in the Bharatanatyam style.

"I can't and I won't. That's stupid!"

"What did you say?" a senior who seemed to be the Leader roared.

Neil looked up defiantly and stood firmly to his ground.

"I'm not frightened of you. I think this is silly – *all* of you are!"

"What cheek!" said a tall and lanky boy with a laugh.

"Stop being cheeky! Do you want to be punished?" said Sanjay, the stocky boy who had met Neil in the corridor that afternoon.

"You think I am scared of *you*? I'm not scared of *anything*! I have seen all sorts of animals at home. I am not *even* scared of them so why should I be scared of you?" Neil reiterated.

Sanjay jumped up from his chair and whispered into Neil's ears:

"Heart. Liver. Kidney!"

"Sorry! What was that?" asked Neil perplexedly.

"Heart–Liver–Kidney!" He said loudly

The others echoed.

"Heart–Liver–Kidney! Heart–Liver–Kidney!!"

Two boys were dispatched to the Biology Laboratory to bring back some preserved anatomical specimens. The three jars containing a dead goat's heart, liver and kidney preserved in formaldehyde were emptied out on the table in the Common Room.

Fumes of formaldehyde from the jar made Neil feel faint. The specimens of a heart, a liver and a kidney were then placed on Neil's hands. He was not aware that they belonged to a dead goat. His hands began to shake and he wanted to vomit. But he simply pursed his lips, outstretched his palms and refused to apologize.

"You saw the graveyard outside the boundary walls when you came up to School, Neil?"

Neil nodded.

"You aren't scared, are you?" said Sanjay who was indeed the leader of the group of senior boys who were ragging Neil.

"Of course, he isn't! Didn't he just say that he was not scared of *anything*?" said a lanky boy.

"OK! Smart Alec! We'll believe you aren't scared of anything if you take a dead man this gift!" Sanjay said.

"Take back his heart, liver and kidney to the dead man! Enter the graveyard and go to the first grave on the right as you enter. The dead man wants his organs back."

Sanjay glared as a boy sniggered and another put his hand in his mouth to control his laughter.

"He is regretting that he donated the organs to our biology lab before he died. He is missing them now. He'll survive with this one kidney – go give him back his organs. He keeps begging for his heart, liver and kidneys..."

"Nonsense!" thought Neil. *"Dead men don't miss their organs! And they definitely don't go around begging for them!"*

"Place the dead man's organs on the gravestone and come back here. We will wait for you and if you are successful we shall declare that you are the Bravest-of-the-brave in St Thomas!"

Neil sighed. He was not going to let on that he was rather nervous by now. The organs in his hand felt yucky!

The moon was full and it lit Neil's path all the way to the graveyard.

He walked with the organs in his palm up to the boundary wall of the School. The seniors gazed through the window expecting the boy to turn around and run back at any moment. But Neil walked on without a backward glance. He exited through a small gate hidden in the compound wall amidst ivy.

The winding path that led to the graveyard was surrounded by trees which hid the moon and cast shadows. As Neil walked along the shadowy path overgrown with grass and ferns, he heard the howl of a wolf. Neil had grown up in the Sal forests of Madhya Pradesh and the sound of wild animals did not scare him.

He entered the graveyard behind the School, turned right and placed the organs in his hands on the first grave. Wiping his icky fingers on the grave stone he folded his hands and said a small prayer for the dead soul.

Neil turned around and headed back to School. As he walked away from the grave he heard a whisper behind him.

"Heart–Liver–Kidney!"

Just then something touched Neil's shoulder. He was startled and ran out of the graveyard with his heart in his mouth.

There was a flutter of wings above his head and he heard a hoot.

"Oh dear! It's only an owl," Neil laughed.

"And that whisper must have been the wind playing tricks with my mind," he thought and sighed with relief.

Neil walked back towards St Thomas School his head held high all set to be titled – the Bravest-of-the-Brave!

He reached that portion of the unkempt path that was hidden amidst shadowy trees. Neil had an ambiguous yet strong feeling that someone was following him. He paused as he heard a rustle.

And then as clear as crystal he heard a deep sonorous voice repeat the words:

"Heart ... Liver ... Kidney!"

"Good Lord! Could it be – no, no it must be the seniors at School. What monkeys they are!" Neil thought to himself.

"Who is there? Who is hiding behind that tree?"

No one responded. Only the sound of the wind through the leaves echoed back to him.

"I *know* you are from St Thomas! Come out whoever it is. I'm not scared of you or anybody. I'm not scared of *anything*!"

Still, there was total silence. An owl hooted from a distant tree.

Neil shrugged his shoulders and walked on to claim his title.

As he walked back he heard the same refrain intermittently:

"Heart–Liver–Kidney! Heart–Liver–Kidney!"

The urgency increased in the voice that followed him with every step Neil took. He hastened his pace and ran as fast as his legs could carry him. The voice followed him just behind his heels.

Neil kept running shouting loudly: "Stop it Sanjay! Stop – *whoever* it is! I'm not scared. I'm *not* scared..."

But the voice did not stop. It followed him right up to the boundary wall of the School: "Heart... Liver... Kidney!"

Breathless and with his heart pounding crazily, Neil entered the School premises. The voice following him stopped! He ran into the Common Room expecting the see all the boys laugh as they saw Sanjay or some other boy entering the room after him, having played a silly practical joke successfully.

Neil stood shell shocked – for there was Sanjay standing in the middle of the room! And so were all the other seven boys who had ragged him earlier that evening. Not a *single* boy was missing from the Common Room.

"So! Who had whispered in the grave yard and harassed me from behind the trees and then again all the way home?" he mused.

Neil saw that the common room was fuller than he had left it. Besides the eight senior boys who had ragged him, there was an irate House Master who was shouting at the pale-faced boys. Some younger boys from Neil's class were also peering in through the common room windows.

Everyone looked around as Neil entered the room – none the worse for his adventure that night.

"He's back! Neil's back!" a shout went up.

The wan faces of the eight older boys relaxed a little. The House Master sighed with relief!

Apparently, soon after Neil had left on his mission the House Master had walked into the common room. He had heard loud peals of laughter even after the bell for proceeding to the dormitories had been rung. A strong smell of formaldehyde had hit him as he entered the room. Seeing the jars from the biology lab, the House Master had ticked off the boys. He threatened them with expulsion and got the eight boys to admit the whole story.

The House Master was just about to send a search party out when Neil had walked into the Common Room.

Neil and the younger boys were immediately sent up to their dormitories to sleep.

Sanjay and the other seven boys who had ragged Neil were expelled from School and sent home. Ragging was totally banned from at St. Thomas Boys' School.

The small side gate opposite the common room was bricked in. Boys of all classes were banned from leaving the School except in groups of four and that too with prior permission of the House Master.

Just before he went to sleep that night, Neil replayed the events of the night in his mind and wondered:

"So, if Sanjay and his friends had been in the Common Room all the time. And if all the St Thomas boys were at School under the watchful eye of the house master, then who did I hear near the grave? Who whispered Heart… Liver… Kidney?"

The whole evening had been bizarre for Neil, who speculated in the dark without any answers.

"Could the seniors have had outside help? Who followed me from the graveyard to the school repeating: Heart… Liver… Kidney?"

No one believed Neil's story. They scoffed at him. He dared everyone to go with him to the grave where he had placed the vital organs at night. The school boys laughed but none of them took up the challenge.

No one from St Thomas School took the path that led to the graveyard. And soon the episode was forgotten.

All was well at St Thomas … or was it?

Two years later on a full moon night, four boys took a shortcut through the graveyard. The sun had set. The boys were on their way back from an outing in the town and were getting late. They hurried past the graves.

As they crossed the last one, they heard a rustle and a hoarse whisper that seemed to say: "Heart... Liver... Kidney!"

On a full moon nights, many a traveler who passes through the graveyard near St Thomas Boys School across Lake Naini in Nainital has heard a hoarse whisper:

"Heart... Liver... Kidney!"

and the soldier marches on –
a headless body without a soul.

VIII

The Headless Soldier

Mussoorie in the foot hills of the Himalayas is known as the Queen of Hills. Built by the British to get away from the unbearable heat of the plains in summer, it has expanded beyond nature's holding capacity over time.

The Headless Soldier first appeared in Mussoorie in the year 1921.

"Where is my head? Give me my head!"

The headless soldier was always elegantly attired in the uniform of the Queen's army. He held a riding crop in one hand and a helmet in the other. The soldier was smartly shod in black riding boots – but he had no head!

He appeared to many in different places at different times…

On cold starless evenings, he was seen riding through the mist on horseback… Before dawn milkmen saw him walking near Rowling Manor above the Cemetery on Camel's Back Road… During the monsoons he appeared on the Mall when it was dark drenched in the rain asking for his head... On moonless nights he was heard dashing across rooftops – the spurs of his boots clattering against the tin roofs. No one went out after sunset for they saw him staring ominously at them in the strangest of places. The whole town talked about the

Headless Soldier in whispers. More often than not he appeared in dreams – or rather nightmares.

Mussoorie was haunted!

Mussoorie centered around The Mall – a road that extended between the Library and Hotel Savoy at one end and the Clock Tower at the other. Most of the Britishers lived in bungalows around the Mall – away from where the dead resided.

The Dead resided in a cemetery situated on Camel's Back Road – a dirt track amidst a dense pine forest on the opposite side of the hill on which the Mall was built. From the side of the cemetery the hill looked like the hump of a camel.

Land was cheaper on Camel's Back road. A few houses had come up by the 1920s when the headless soldier first appeared...

Rowling Manor was located on the hillside above Camel's Back road. Captain Rowling's house had sprawling gardens and an outhouse. The staff quarters were at the rear of the Manor.

Captain Rowling liked his liquor but could not hold it. He also had a liver condition but always had a strong opinion about liquor.

"Rum! Now that is the drink for a man – a real man!"

His wife, Jane Rowling could do nothing but nod her head for the Captain could easily fly off into a violent rage when he was drunk.

Jane was a pretty *Pahadan* – a girl-from-the-hills – from Tehri Garhwal. She was named Janaki at birth. Her parents had died when she was an infant. Her grandmother was poor and had left Janaki at the doorstep of Waverly Convent.

The nuns at Waverly adopted the child and called her Jane. By the time she finished School she had the bearing of a lady.

Groomed by the Nuns, Jane had acquired table manners and the correct etiquette of the times.

Jane was working as a Nurse at the Hospital in Mussoorie where Captain Rowling had been admitted with an inflamed liver. The prognosis was bad. He was in the hospital for two months and barely survived. Jane had nursed the ailing Captain back to health. Theirs was a quick romance.

Captain Rowling married Nurse Jane in the small chapel inside the hospital premises. The nuns from Waverly were in attendance.

The Captain swore off liquor and took an early retirement from the army. He decided to trade in timber which was by then a good business. The couple settled down in Mussoorie at Rowling Manor.

The Rowlings were not accepted by the blue-nosed uppity British Society of Mussoorie. Much to Jane's distress, the Captain did not want to socialize with the nuns who had brought her up. Nor did he have any desire to mingle with either the Indian or the small Anglo-Indian community of Mussoorie. Captain and Jane Rowling had no friends in town.

The Rowlings were quite the social outcasts and lived a quiet life near the graveyard on Camels Back.

Quiet – except when the Captain drank too much ...

Five years after they were married, when Paul their older son was four years old and Peter was two, Captain Rowling started to drink again. In a drunken state he became acrimonious and abusive and no longer cared whether his children were watching. Over time, he started to drink heavily every night. The more he drank the louder he shouted...

"Rum! *More* Rum! Hurry up you fool!"

The Captain would fly into a rage when his wife reminded him about his liver. Jane had learnt to maintain a distance when he drank himself silly. She often had an early supper with the children while the staff at the Manor served the Captain his drink and dinner.

One foggy Sunday evening the Captain got particularly violent. He hit Jagdish the *'Chhota Bearer'* with his riding crop in a fit of drunken rage and kicked him with his boots till the boy fainted.

Jagdish was an earnest young lad, barely seventeen years of age. He had come from a village beyond Tehri as an apprentice to his father's older brother Ram Lal, the *'Head Bearer'* of Rowling Manor. Ram Lal patiently tried to train his nephew but the boy was scared stiff of Captain *Sahab*.

The minute the Captain raised his voice the poor lad would be all thumbs! No wonder when the Captain hollered for his fifth glass of rum that Sunday evening, Jagdish started shivering nervously.

He forgot to put on his gloves, forgot to cover the tray with a cloth and spilled the Captain's rum on his favorite tray – an exquisite piece made up of rosewood with exquisitely carved roses on the edges. The Captain had brought it with him along with the other knick-knacks from England and he loved it.

Captain Rowling flew into an uncontrollable rage and thrashed the boy till he fainted.

No one dared interfere – least of all Jane!

The Captain shouted for the 'Head Bearer' who was aghast to see his nephew beaten up black and blue.

"Take this lazy good-for-nothing back to your village. Leave him behind. I have no use for him!"

Ram Lal pursed his lips and picked up Jagdish up with a grim face.

"But *you* come back soon! Bring a smart well-trained boy with you this time," the Captain directed further.

The Head Bearer of Rowling Manor left for his village with his nephew the next morning and never came back.

A week later news arrived that Jagdish had developed high fever after reaching the village. Four days later he had passed away.

All the other servants left their jobs at Rowling Manor stern-facedly: the two gardeners, the stable hand, the watchman, the parlor maid, the children's nanny and the cook. They said nothing to Captain Rowling – but in their minds they all blamed him for Jagdish's death.

All left except Bhola, the squat and burly washer man. Unlike the other staff at the Manor, Bhola was not from the hills. He was from Gorakhpur in the plains and had never quite got along with the other staff who were all hill folk.

A week later Captain Rowling died.

The night the Captain died Jane and the Rowling boys were alone in the Manor. The washer man Bhola was the lone servant in the staff quarters.

The Captain was buried in the Cemetery on Camel's Back Road in Mussoorie on a cold and misty morning on November, 22,1922.

No one witnessed Captain Rowling's burial except Mrs. Rowling and Bhola. The Mussoorie rumor mill had it that the Captain had drunk himself to his grave. No one came to condole. The Rowlings had no friends – no one really cared!

Captain Rowling had left a tidy sum for his widow and the boys in the Bank. The timber trade had done well. Soon all was well at Rowling Manor. New staff joined – a cook, a bearer, a nanny and a gardener. The death of Captain Rowling was soon forgotten.

And then the Headless Soldier appeared – walking under the pine trees near Rowling Manor in the mist...

One frosty morning three weeks before Christmas, a milkman who supplied milk at the Savoy saw an apparition in the forest. It was foggy so he could only see a silhouette near the cemetery on Camel's Back road. He shook as he retold the story the umpteenth time.

"It was a soldier! A *headless* one... I saw him with my own eyes."

No one believed the milkman. But *he* knew what he had seen.

"Rubbish! There is no such thing!" was the general refrain.

A few days later the *Headless Soldier* stopped by the kitchen window at Rowling Manor before dinner and demanded his head in a loud sonorous voice.

"Where is my head? I want my head back!"

The cook fainted.

As soon as she came around she literally ran out of the Manor and into the night without even waiting to pick up her belongings...

"Bhoot Bhoot – Ghost, ghost!" she shouted in fear.

Mussoorie was abuzz with all sorts of stories.

Rowling Manor soon acquired the notorious reputation of being a '*Bhoot Bangala* – a Ghost House'.

All the servants left the Manor the day after the headless *bhoot* demanded his head from the Cook – all but Bhola, the faithful washer man. And once again there was no one but

Bhola, Jane Rowling and the two young Rowling boys in the large Manor.

For two years the situation at Rowling Manor was similar to the one that had existed for a week just before Captain Rowling had passed away.

Over time Bhola became Jane Rowling's *Man Friday*.

Two years later Mrs. Kailash K Srivastava arrived from Allahabad.

The Rowling boys, Paul and Peter, were nine and seven when Kailash Srivastava first took up residence at the Manor. Mrs. Jane Rowling had advertised for a live-in governess. Kailash was a mathematics graduate from Crosthwaite College and belonged to a forward-looking family of Allahabad. Jane liked her and told her to move into the outhouse of Rowling Manor.

The horse-drawn cart driver who had brought Kailash to the Manor had looked at her and her baggage in disbelief, as she gave him the address she wanted to be taken to.

"You want to go to the Rowling's '*Bhoot Bangla*'? – to stay there? But *why*? No one goes there!"

"Rowlings Manor on Camel's Back Road, like I said before! And there are no such things as ghosts. How can there be a ghost house? It's all utter nonsense!" Kailash had laughed.

On arrival Bhola showed the governess her rooms in the outhouse. He carried her suitcases in and informed her that he was the Bearer of the Manor. After unpacking, Kailash walked across to the main house. Mrs. Jane Rowling had asked her to have her first supper at the Manor.

Dusk had fallen when Kailash entered the dining hall. The room was dark and empty. The sun had set but the candles had not yet been lit. Possibly a window was open somewhere for the fog had entered and the room was dark and cold.

Kailash looked at the grandfather clock and saw that she had arrived too early – in fact an hour before the appointed time. She pulled at the bell rope but it did not ring. So, she stuck her head out of the door.

"Bearer! *Bearer*!" Kailash called out.

From somewhere in the night she heard footsteps and a voice.

"Coming Madam!"

Kailash sat down on a sofa by the window. She heard someone enter and looked up with a smile expecting to see Bhola. Instead she saw a younger boy immaculately attired in the spotless white uniform of a bearer. He wore pure white gloves. His face was hidden in the shadows. The young bearer held out a beautiful tray neatly covered with a sparkling white tray cloth – Captain Rowling's favorite tray of rosewood with exquisitely carved roses on its edges ...

Her smile froze at what Kailash saw – or thought she saw – the bearer carrying on the tray.

She couldn't see too well in the dark ... but it could not be ... it simply could not be true!

Kailash gagged when she saw that what was placed at the center of the rosewood tray was indeed a *Decapitated Human Head*!

Her heart missed a beat and then started to race like seven crazy horses... She could scarcely breathe!

Kailash was overcome by nausea and she bent over and vomited all over the rug on the wooden floor. She kept retching for what seemed like eternity – and then collapsed on the floor.

The sound of footsteps heralded the arrival of the hefty Bhola.

"Madam! Madam! What is it? What happened Madam?"

Seeing Bhola, Kailash took in short breaths and muttered some gibberish. He helped her up to the sofa and gave her some water. Then he quickly lit the candles on the table beside her.

She gasped for breath and whispered: "Look. Look!... See..."

Kailash pointed out in the general direction of the door from which a young liveried bearer had walked in a few minutes earlier with a tray bearing a human head.

"What Madam? *Where* Madam? What is it?"

Kailash saw that there was nothing – *nothing* but the evening mist! A window had been left open by mistake and cold wisps of mist were entering the room.

Bhola closed the window and removed the soiled carpet. He then ignited the fire in the fire place and lit the candelabra up. The room began to look warmer and friendlier.

Once the mist was shut out and the room was lit up, Kailash could scarcely believe what she had imagined she had seen. It was *too* grotesque!

She began to wonder whether she had allowed the mist and the dark shadows in the room to play on her mind.

"What a long day this has been! And I do have a wild imagination. That's what it must be ... Just my mind playing games!" she mused.

She felt both comforted and rather foolish at the same time.

"The Cart Driver had also called the place a 'Bhoot Bangla' ... and then this spooky room in the mist! ... Yes, that's what it was – just my imagination!"

"Jane Madam will come down in half an hour. Please have a

drink in the meantime. What would you like to drink?" Bhola asked.

She saw Bhola walk across the room to a cabinet at the other end.

And *there* it lay on top of the cabinet near a half-finished bottle...

A beautiful tray made up of rosewood with exquisitely carved roses on the edges, neatly covered with a pure white tray cover – just as she had seen in the bearer's hand!

Mrs. Kailash K Srivastava jumped up with a start.

"It was *not* my imagination!" She cried as she ran towards the tray.

"I saw a head! A *human* head on this tray – I saw it! I know I did..."

Kailash saw the look on Bhola's face before he lowered his eyes.

"He knows – of course he knows!" she thought.

Just then Mrs. Jane Rowling came down the stairs into the dining area. She looked nervous and as pale as a ghost as she looked first at Mrs. Srivastava and then at Bhola and finally at the tray...

Kailash saw the look Jane and Bhola exchanged.

"They both know! What are the two of them hiding?" she mused.

"What is it? What did I see? Tell me – tell me *all*!" she said aloud.

Kailash turned to Jane Rowling accusingly.

"I know you *both* know! I just saw a liveried bearer bring that tray in... Tell me how the tray that's lying there had a *head* on it – a *human* head?"

Kailash shuddered as she remembered the horrendous sight.

"I *saw* it – I saw it with these eyes!"

She gesticulated agitatedly with her hands. Jane and Bhola looked on silently.

"I will pack my bags *this* minute and leave right now!"

Kailash stomped her feet and wagged her finger threateningly.

"You better tell me *all*... Else I'll take you to the Police!"

Jane looked across at Bhola and tried to calm Kailash down.

"No wait. Please wait Mrs. Srivastava. I will tell you *all* ... We *both* will tell you all!"

Jane took Kailash's hands in her own and urged her to sit down next to her on the sofa. She looked deeply into her eyes and sighed...

"You are right Mrs. Srivastava. You *saw* what you saw. The mist and your own imagination were not playing tricks with your mind."

Jane spoke nervously her voice soft and face worried. She looked beseechingly at Bhola as if to ask to help her. The stocky man patted the back of Jane's hand gently and he pulled a chair to sit closer to the sofa.

"Oh my God! They are in this together! Collaborators in crime – or whatever this is... but these two definitely share a secret. Bhola is certainly more than a washer man or a bearer or whatever Jane Rowling calls him... Over the years they have come to mean more to each other than they want the world to know!"

Kailash pushed her thoughts away as she heard Bhola exclaim.

"Yes Madam! That's true – Madam Jane is right! Your eyes were not misleading you... What you saw was *indeed* this very tray being carried in by Jagdish."

"*Jagdish*?" asked Kailash in a high tone, rather perplexed.

"Jagdish used to be the '*Chhota* Bearer' of Rowling Manor until he died two years ago – a few days after Captain Rowling beat him up and sent him home."

Bhola paused to see if the governess was following his story so far.

"This Jagdish… You say he died two years ago. So, why do I *still* see him? Or what is it that I see?"

"You *did* see the apparition of the *Chhota* Bearer of the Manor carrying Captain Rowling's head on his favorite tray…"

"I saw *what*? – the severed head of a man on a tray carried by a *specter*? Now *that* is simply bizarre!"

Kailash was flabbergasted at the prospect.

"Good Lord! A *phantom* carrying a decapitated head?…"

Bhola and Jane looked at her with unease and then at each other. In the soft glow of the candles their gaze appeared meaningful – as if they had shared many a secret…

"*We* see him too – both Madam and I," Bhola said softly.

"Yes, we do!" added Jane.

"Every evening as dusk falls and the mist descends and enters this room, Jagdish's ghost arrives through that door. He carries Captain Rowling's severed head into the dining room on that tray. Before he and the head disappear, the specter places the tray next to the Captain's bottle of rum lying unfinished since he passed away two years ago."

Kailash gaped at Bhola in amazement.

"Yes. We see him *every* day!" Jane added.

Kailash turned towards Jane and shot a volley of questions…

"You *do*? And you aren't scared? And what about your sons?"

"The boys don't see anything. Only the Bearer and I have been seeing Jagdish – and now you have too. And no, I'm not scared. He doesn't say anything to any of us. Every evening he walks in with the rosewood tray and then disappears in the mist – as does the Captain's head and..."

Bhola cut Jane short with a retort.

"Why should *we* be scared? He's not angry with *us*. It's the Captain who hit Jagdish. Madam Jane was always good to him. So why should he trouble us?"

"Yes. And the boys do not see him. Just the Bearer and I do."

Jane urged Bhola to go ahead with the rest of the story with her eyes and Bhola complied.

"No one else sees the head of the Captain besides the two of us. You Madam Srivastava are the first!"

"People in Mussoorie see the phantom of a headless soldier in search of his head..."

"And we at the Manor see the Captain's Head!" Bhola added.

"Yes, brought in on a rosewood tray every evening after the sun sets by another phantom!" Jane elaborated.

That night between the two of them Bhola and Jane unraveled the remaining pieces of the obscure esoteric jigsaw bit by bit...

Jane narrated how Jagdish had died in his village after he had been beaten up the drunk Captain in a rage and how all the servants, except Bhola the faithful, had left the Manor – and how a week later a stranger arrived at the Manor looking for a job on the fateful Sunday when Captain Rowling died.

The stranger who arrived asking for a job was about twenty years of age. Jane was rather pleased to see the young boy. She was exhausted with all the household chores she had been performing ever since all the servants had left after Jagdish died.

"I am Prakash, Madam Rowling. I can cook whatever you

want me to. Roast chicken ... mashed potatoes... Whatever you say!" he said with folded hands and a broad smile.

Jane smiled back and asked: "Aren't you too young to be a cook? Where have you learnt to cook *our* kind of food?"

"I am an understudy at Hotel Savoy Madam. The Head Cook is my mother's real brother. I've learnt how to cook from him."

"What references do you..."

Prakash in his eagerness cut Jane's question short.

"My father Ram Lal has worked for you. He was your head bearer Madam. Jagdish the *chhota* bearer was my cousin,"

Jane was pleased. Ram Lal was trustworthy even though he had not come back to work at the Manor after his nephew's death. She engaged Prakash, his son.

"OK. Take over right away!"

Jane gladly took off the apron she was wearing.

"I have made some soup and toast for the children's supper. I will share it with them" she said adding: "Captain Rowling is out riding. He will be back in about an hour. Make him a decent supper!"

Jane took stock of the pantry and showed Prakash where the raw material and the condiments were kept.

"Ah! So, do a roast chicken with baked potatoes and peas."

She opened a drawer where the knives and other cutlery was kept in the kitchen. The carving knife appeared to be blunt. Prakash took it out and felt the edge and then turned to her.

"Don't worry Madam. I will sharpen it on a wet stone. I know how to. I also have my own set of kitchen knives."

Jane looked at her brilliant find and sighed with relief.

"What a Godsend!" She thought as she walked out to the dining area to show her new cook-cum-bearer the liquor cabinet.

"The Captain likes his rum before dinner."

Jane held up a half empty bottle of rum and showed Prakash the Captain's favorite rosewood tray with carved roses on the edges.

"The rum goes on this tray."

Then Jane picked out a white linen tray cloth edged with lace.

"But don't forget the tray cloth – and your gloves," she added as she handed the tray to the boy.

"And *please* pour carefully. Do not spill any!" she urged her new Cook-cum-Bearer recalling the plight of poor Jagdish.

After an early supper Jane went upstairs to tuck the boys into bed.

"The Captain should be here soon," she thought once the boys were asleep.

She strained to hear the sound of horse's hooves signaling the Captain's return. There was complete silence. She could not even hear the clutter of pans. Jane went down to the kitchen to investigate.

Everything seemed to be in order. A pleasant aroma was emanating from the stove. The dining table was set properly. The fire was glowing in the fireplace and the candles were lit. The rosewood tray with carved roses was lying on the liquor cabinet neatly covered with a white cloth.

Jane sighed with relief. She could now put her feet up and relax.

"Bearer! Bearer! Where are you?"

She looked for Prakash to tell him that she was going upstairs to rest until the Captain came home. But he wasn't in the house. She looked out of the window and saw the boy vigorously sharpening a carving knife for the roast chicken. The sharpened edge of the knife gleamed in the moonlight. The shiny blade looked sharper than she had ever seen it.

Jane smiled and took one last look at the dining table. Satisfied with the preparations, she walked up the stairs. She soaked her feet in warm water and then lay down to take a short nap. Soon she slipped into a deep sleep.

The sky was the color of ashes of roses when Jane opened her eyes. The snowy mountain peaks had a rosy hue. She jumped out of bed with a start. It was almost dawn. She had slept through the night!

"What will the Captain say?"

Jane looked at the other side of the bed. It had not been slept on. She walked across to Captain Rowling's study where he had a sofa that he slept on when he drank too late. The room was empty. She went to the children's room. The boys were fast asleep.

"Where is Captain Rowling? Didn't he come home last night?"

Jane panicked. She ran down the stairs. Her mind racing faster than ever as she stumbled on the last stair.

"What could have happened? Had he met with an accident?"

She rang the bell for Prakash, the new Bearer-cum-Cook but there was no response.

Through the window Jane could see the faithful Bhola hanging some washing on the clothesline in the backyard.

"No point calling out to him." She thought. *"He's too far to hear."*

She walked into the living-cum-dining room to see if the Captain was having his tea early. The sun's rays were just entering the room through the slats in the windows. There was a dark shadowy patch near the liquor cabinet in the corner of the room.

Jane looked at the cabinet and was shocked at what she saw on next to Captain Rowling's unfinished bottle of rum.

The cloth covering the rosewood tray was blood-stained and held the Captain's severed head...

Jane screamed hysterically. Bhola rushed indoors just in time to catch her shuddering body before she fell to the ground in a faint. He quickly laid Jane on the sofa and ran outdoors to grab the washed bedsheet from the clothesline.

"No woman should see this gory sight! Least of all Madam Jane!"

Bhola thought about how kind Jane had been to him and to the entire staff as he wrapped the Captain's decapitated head in the bedsheet. He rushed out to the garden and went to the deep pit he had been digging in the back yard for making manure from dead fallen leaves.

On a foggy November morning in 1922 Bhola buried the severed head of Captain Rowling – wrapped in a bed-sheet in the pit under the large silver oak at Rowling Manor.

The clock struck five as Bhola returned to the main house. He cleaned the place up and gave Jane a large shot of brandy to calm her nerves. There was a great deal to be done.

The boy Prakash who Jane had hired the earlier evening as the new Cook-cum-Bearer had vanished. He had taken the one small bundle he had brought with him. There was no sign that he had ever even come to the Manor.

There was no point going to the Police. The Captain had been murdered gruesomely. Bhola and Jane would be the prime suspects. There was no murder weapon and no one but the two of them had seen Prakash arrive at the Manor. Peter and Paul, the boys, had seen him briefly the night before but they were too young to be reliable witnesses before a Court of Law.

And the decapitated head of the Captain had already been buried at dawn by Bhola.

There was nothing more to do – but to bury Captain Rowling's headless body before anyone saw it. Bhola lost no time in building a rough coffin from trunks of pine trees that he had been lopped a few days ago for firewood. Jane helped Bhola wrap the Captain's body in a shroud made up of bed sheets. They put the rough coffin on the horse drawn cart and rode the cart to the cemetery. Bhola dug up a shallow grave.

The body of Captain Rowling was buried at six in the morning of November, 22, 1922 in the cemetery on Camel's Back Road amidst a thick pine forest without any fuss.

The head had already been buried earlier that morning below a silver oak tree at Rowling Manor.

Bhola and Jane reached the Manor before the boys arose and demanded their breakfast. Captain Rowling's death was a non-event. The few townsmen who had seen the Captain ride into town on Sundays had seen him more drunk than sober. He had no friends. Nobody missed Captain Rowling in Mussoorie!

Ten days later on a foggy morning, a milkman took a short cut through the cemetery on Camels Back Road. Winter had set in. The sky was a hazy rose-pink. Through the dense fog the milkman saw a silhouette in the pine forest. He stood transfixed as he saw an apparition that appeared to be headless.

Since then the specter of a Headless Soldier walks through the hills of Mussoorie seeking his head...

"Where is my head? Give me back my head!"

Every evening at dusk the liveried ghost of the *chhota* bearer walks up to the liquor cabinet with a rosewood tray with carved roses and places it next to an unfinished bottle of rum...

And the Headless Soldier's Head is carried in to Rowling Manor.

About the Author

Rajni Sekhri Sibal is a writer and a civil servant. From Poem to Prose, Rajni connects with people with a sensitive heart that respects human dignity. Her writings span serious matters like disaster management to lyrical poems about life in all its facets. She creates an enthralling experience for readers and touches their lives with her words.

All this, while being a member of the Indian Administrative Service. Rajni is the first lady to top the civil services examination. She has formulated and implemented government policies in diverse fields like agriculture, industry, education, finance, skill development and disaster management. She rose to be Secretary to the Government of India and is the recipient of multiple accolades including the Indian of the Year award for her courage and commitment.

Rajni has authored two anthologies of enchanting verses: 'Clouds End and Beyond' and 'Fragrant Words'. Three of her published books – *Tours and Inspections for Effective Monitoring, Kamadhenu* and *Are You Prepared for a Disaster?* – evolved from the work she was doing at that time at the Academy, in the Ministry of Agriculture and the Ministry of Home Affairs, respectively.

The Haunting Himalayas is the author's first collection of esoteric stories set against the backdrop of pine forests and quaint towns and villages nestled in the Himalayas.